BACK TO THE FUTURE

New Urbanism and the
Rise of Neotraditionalism in Urban Planning

Edited by

Karl Besel and Viviana Andreescu

University Press of America,® Inc.
Lanham · Boulder · New York · Toronto · Plymouth, UK

Copyright © 2013 by
University Press of America,® Inc.
4501 Forbes Boulevard
Suite 200
Lanham, Maryland 20706
UPA Acquisitions Department (301) 459-3366

10 Thornbury Road
Plymouth PL6 7PP
United Kingdom

Library of Congress Control Number: 2013940733
ISBN: 978-0-7618-6165-2 (paperback : alk. paper)
eISBN: 978-0-7618-6166-9

Cover photograph: Village of West Clay, Carmel, Indiana.
By Viviana Andreescu.

Karl Besel

This book is dedicated to my lovely wife Ashley and my beautiful daughter Lily. Thank you for your patience, flexibility, and suggestions. I could not have completed this project without your support, including your willingness to organize and embark upon a variety of travels and adventures.

Viviana Andreescu

In fond memory of my parents, Mara and Nicolae Andreescu.

To my dear friends, Lorelei and Sandi Blada, city lovers and enthusiast international travelers. Thank you for your encouragements and for always being there for me.

Contents

List of Figures

List of Tables

Acknowledgements

A major part of this book is based on primary data obtained through surveys and in-depth interviews. The editors and authors involved in the writing of this manuscript are extremely grateful to the city mayors, housing developers, urban planners, realtors, active citizens, and new urbanism advocates who shared their experience, expertise, and time with us. Without their willingness to help, this project would not have been possible.

Thanks to Randy A. Simes, city planner and new urbanism enthusiast, for providing the inspiration for the cover photograph. Brenwick developers George Sweet and Tom Huston took a risk in building this new urbanist community on the west side of Carmel. It was the first of its kind within the state and now, the rest of the country is taking notice of their success, as witnessed by a September, 2012 article in Money Magazine that ranked Carmel as the "best small city" winner. One of the factors that pushed Carmel to the top of the list was the variety of home options available to both younger families and empty nesters in several innovative developments, including the Village of West Clay.

We would also like to thank our undergraduate and graduate students for their insights and pertinent suggestions. In particular, we thank Brandy Kizer, who competently produced some of the graphs and tables included in this book.In addition, a number of Indiana University faculty members and staff, including Cherie Dodd, Kathy Ross, and Krista Stamps provided technical and editing assistance during the last phase of this project. Their expertise and efficiency in handling these matters allowed us to bring this project into fruition in a timely manner and we thank them for all their help. We also want to acknowledge the funding support received from a variety of grants, including the Indiana University Exploration Traveling Grants fund.

We owe special thanks and gratitude to Laura Espinoza, our kind and patient book editor from University Press of America, who offered invaluable guidance, helped us correct our mistakes, and shepherded with professionalism this project to completion. Most importantly, we would like to thank our family members for their support, devotion, and continuous encouragements throughout the process of writing this book.

Introduction

Viviana Andreescu and Karl Besel

For the past six decades, Americans have left the cities behind and steadily moved to the suburbs. It seems however, as one scholar recently noted, that "the pendulum is swinging back toward urban living, and there are many reasons to believe this swing will continue."[1] The US subprime-mortgage crisis that eventually led up to the late-2000s financial crisis intensified problems in many communities, contributing to the decline of many suburban neighborhoods all over America. Recent research suggests that a structural transformation is under way in the housing market and that the American metropolitan residential patterns and cultural preferences are gradually changing. According to C. Leinberger, the Charles Bendit Distinguished Scholar and Research Professor at George Washington University School of Business, in demand today are mixed-income, walkable cities and suburbs that will support the knowledge economy, promote environmental sustainability and create jobs.[2]

Back to the Future explores different aspects of contemporary urban living, as well as the recent changes in Americans' attitudes toward public spaces, urban centers, and even suburban sprawl; the book also discusses the challenges architects, planners, urban designers, developers, entrepreneurs, and city leaders have been and will be facing in the near future when trying to select policies and actions that would best serve the entire community. By using specific examples from old and new urban and suburban communities within the Midwest and the South, we hope to contribute new knowledge to the debate on planning and urban design theories and the way their application to real-life settings can influence the quality of life in revitalized inner-city neighborhoods and also in the new non-conventional suburbs. In particular, our discussion focuses on "new urbanism," an urban design movement that over the course of the past two decades managed to reform many aspects of real estate development, urban planning, and municipal land-use strategies.

Founded in 1993 by a group of enthusiastic American architects, the organizing body for new urbanism is the Congress for the New Urbanism (CNU). CNU has gradually become an influential multi-disciplinary organization that supports the creation of sustainable, walkable, mixed-use neighborhoods that provide for better health and economic outcomes. Working against the conventional, mainly sprawl-oriented dogma of the post-WWII period, supporters of the new urban design movement advocate the restructuring of public policy and development practices to make cities and towns more engaging, vibrant and livable. In particular, as outlined in the preamble of CNU's Charter, the new urbanists support the restoration of existing urban centers and towns within coherent metropolitan regions and argue that community, economics, environment, health and design need to be addressed simultaneously through urban design and planning. In addition, "new urbanism stands for the reconfiguration of sprawling suburbs into communities of real neighborhoods and diverse districts, the conservation of natural environments, and the preservation of our built legacy."[3]

Disapproved by some and praised by others, new urbanism remains a controversial theory of urban planning and only the future will determine the viability and the generalizability of its principles. History will decide if the new urbanism's contribution to city planning will remain almost purely stylistic, or if the new urban design movement will be able to truly change the basic pattern of suburban development. Our intention is to stimulate discussion and to present novel information that could contribute to the literature on new urbanism and to a better understanding of the direct and indirect outcomes when new urbanist principles are applied in urban and suburban developments.

In many ways the planning philosophy embraced by the new urbanists is not entirely new, representing in most part a return to the neighborhood developments that characterized the pre-automobile age. Therefore, the first chapters of this book intend to identify the roots of new urbanism and also to offer a brief historical overview of planning strategies and housing policies that shaped the (sub)urban landscape in US in the last sixty years and created the conditions for change and partial return to planning and design models, which many continue to perceive as being successful in serving the public interest.

Considering the fact that the proponents of the new urbanism movement were not the first to criticize the modernist planning techniques that have been put into practice in United States after WWII, the first two chapters of the book are focusing on two American thinkers whose ideas strongly influenced the new urbanism movement. One of them is Lewis Mumford, a social philosopher and historian, who strongly criticized the 'anti-urban' development of post-war America and who believed that cities should be characterized by beauty, order, spaciousness, and clarity of purpose. The other precursor of new urbanism briefly discussed in this book is Jane Jacobs. A writer and an activist interested in communities and urban planning, Jacobs published more than half a century ago a greatly influential book (*The Death and Life of Great American Cities*), where she called for planners to reconsider the single-use housing projects, large car-dependent thoroughfares, and segregated commercial centers that were the norm at the time. In order to see to what extent Mumford's and Jacobs's perceptions of the Americans' spatial preferences were valid, the second chapter of the book also includes an empirical analysis of data collected from a probability sample of residents of Louisville, Kentucky. Although the sample used in this analysis is not representative for the entire US urban population, the study could offer some information about the Americans' perceptions and preferences regarding the urban environment at the beginning of the new millennium.

The third chapter of the book (*We're on a Road to Nowhere: Housing Policy in the U.S.*) offers a brief historical overview of the American housing policy and discusses the policy influences on post-war suburban sprawl. In addition, the chapter identifies the factors that contributed to a paradigm shift and presents the recent changes in US housing policies. The fourth chapter of the book (*A Case for Traditional Town Planning*) compares conventional suburban planning strategies with traditional town planning (found in the City of Alexandria, Virginia or in Georgetown, DC) that served as models for the neotraditional planning of the new urbanism communities. The chapter highlights the advantages offered by different elements of planning and design found in older (pre-WWII) urban neighborhoods and also in modern towns built in accordance with the new urbanism principles.

Chapter five (*Louisville's Historical Belles: Cherokee Triangle and Old Louisville*) is closely related to the topics presented in the fourth chapter of the book. It includes a more detailed presentation of two inner-city historical neighborhoods that for almost one century managed to maintain a relatively high market value, are perceived by most Louisvillians as highly desirable, and are now serving as inspiration for regional new urbanism developments, such as Norton Commons in Kentucky.

The following chapters of the book present several case studies, which critically examine new urbanism communities established in relatively conservative and risk-averse housing markets in the Midwest and the American South. Chapter six (*A Tale of Two Villages: Park DuValle and West Clay*) includes a comparison of two new urbanism communities recently developed in Kentucky and Indiana in two neighborhoods that have different socio-demographic and spatial characteristics (i.e., one represents an example of an inner-city revitalization project, while the other exemplifies a non-conventional suburban development). The chapter provides information about the projects' beginnings, obstacles encountered by local leaders who supported these developments and the market response when the projects were finalized. Chapter seven (*New Urbanism in a University Town: The Case of Gainesville and the University of Florida*), as the title suggests, includes a case study of new urbanism projects in a university town in Florida. The development processes of two residential subdivisions (Haile Plantation & Town of Tioga) are discussed in detail. In addition, the authors present the benefits and the limitations associated with this type of new urbanism communities.

With the application of the new urbanism principles (e.g., walkability, connectivity, mixed-use and density, mixed housing, quality architecture and urban design, traditional neighborhood structure, increased population density, green transportation, and sustainability), the ultimate objective of the new urbanism perspective is to increase the residents' quality of life. Based on interviews conducted with residents in two different communities from Tennessee (a conventional suburban neighborhood developed in the late 1980s/early 1990s and a neotraditional suburban neighborhood designed in accordance with the principles of new urbanism approximately two decades later) and on a thorough examination of other scholarly studies focusing on the same topic, the authors of chapter eight (*Building Community: Residential Satisfaction in Conventional and Neotraditional Suburban Neighborhoods*) tried to determine if the application of the new urbanism principles did indeed contribute to an increased sense of community and to a higher level of residential satisfaction. Although it appears that neotraditional suburban neighborhoods foster a stronger sense of community than conventional suburban neighborhoods, more research is needed to clearly determine if the new urbanist communities are generating significantly higher levels of residential satisfaction and an improved quality of life.

Chapter nine (*Best Businesses for New Urbanism Communities*) attempts to address a topic seldom discussed in analyses of new urbanism communities. Based on document analysis, direct observation, and in-depth interviews conducted in five neo-traditional communities located in Kentucky, Indiana, and Florida, the author of this chapter provides information about the business activity and types of businesses in the (urban and suburban) locations under study and identifies factors more likely to predict business failure or survival when mixed-use developments are undertaken.

The final chapter of the book offers a synthesis of the knowledge imparted in the book. In addition, the authors of this chapter offer suggestions and recommendations aimed primarily at those directly involved in the production of urban spaces from a new urbanist perspective.

Notes

1. C. Leinberger, *The Next Slum?* (The Atlantic Online, March 2008).

2. C. Leinberger, *The Death of the Fringe Suburb* (The New York Times, November 26, 2011, p. A19).

3. The mission statement of the Congress for New Urbanism and CNU's Charter are available at: http://www.cnu.org/history. In 1996, the US Environmental Protection Agency joined with several non-profit and governmental organizations to form the Smart Growth Network. The ten principles that guide the Smart Growth Movement are available at: http://www.smartgrowth.org.

Chapter One

The City in History: Mumford Revisited

Karl Besel and Viviana Andreescu

In a book that attempted to put new urbanism in historical context, Emily Talen (2005) contended that the new urban reform movement that gained prominence in the 1990s combined multiple inter-related traditions, each having specific sets of cultural biases and sometimes, opposing ideals. According to Talen, the four "urbanist cultures" that exemplify different approaches to city making in America are: *Incrementalism* (focus on small scale improvements and incremental change), *Plan-making* (stresses the importance of using plans to achieve good urbanism), *Planned communities* (focus on complete settlements), and *Regionalism* (focus on the city in its natural regional context). Talen argues that from the perspective of New Urbanism, all four cultures have values and need to be incorporated in the promotion of urbanism in America. In Talen's view, urbanism is "the vision and the quest to achieve the best possible human settlement (...) operating within the context of certain established principles." And the principles about the built environment, which are recurrent and embedded in the American consciousness, are diversity, equity, community, connectivity, and the importance of civil and public space. Accordingly, new urbanism "seeks to promote qualities that urban reformers have always sought: vital, beautiful, just, environmentally benign human settlements."[1]

This chapter will present some of the influential ideas of Lewis Mumford, a proponent of the peripheral planned communities in America, whose quest for an ideal urban environment lasted decades. Lewis Mumford, whose book, *The City in History*, won the 1962 National Book Award for nonfiction was "a towering American intellectual with an international reputation," who continues to be regarded as "the leading 20th century authority on cities — their history design and communal purpose." Writer, journalist, critic and academician, Mumford (1895-1990) was the author of more than 20 books and 1,000 articles and reviews, on subjects ranging from art and literature to the histories of technology and urbanism.[2] In 1955, Lewis Mumford was elected to the American Academy of Arts and Letters and in 1964 he received the United States Presidential Medal of Freedom. A contemporary of Mumford, the American writer Malcom Cawley, called Lewis Mumford "the last of the great humanists"[3] and Miller (1989) contended that Mumford produced a body of work almost unequaled in the twentieth century for its range and richness.[4] Although, as Talen (2008) observed, the "historical lineage of New Urbanism is often narrowly limited to the traditional town-planning techniques of John Nolen and Raymond Unwin," Mumford's views on the city, urbanism and regionalism in particular, in addition to the ideas formulated in the 1920s by other core members of the Regional Planning Association of America (RPAA)[5], such as Clarence Stein, Benton MacKaye, Alexander Bing, and Henry Wright can be considered the "historical basis of the regional, polycentric city concepts that are an essential part of the New Urbanist manifesto."[6] Organized and led by C. Stein in 1923, RPAA was an urban reform association that through its ten-year existence formulated a new vision of the urban communities and regions by creating city building policies, regional settlement frameworks, open space preservation strategies, large-scale building policies, and building prototypes.[7] In sum, RPAA managed to successfully conceptualize, experiment, and influence the way cities, architecture, and planning in America would be perceived.[8] Even if, as Luccarelli (1995) observed, outside of urban planning circles RPAA might be a little known chapter in American history, the pragmatic creativity of RPAA and the fact that it presented a viable alternative to megalopolis should be noted. By placing conservation of land and landscape into the context of new urban forms, RPAA's plans for 'regional cities' and managed decentralization took modern technologies into account and addressed the social inequities created by industrialization and capital accumulation.[9] Regionalism, the focus of Mumford's work in the 1920s and 1930s, "was the principle that united three ideas: *neotechnics* — the adaptation of new technologies for the purpose of restoring the natural environment; *organicism* — the restoration of nature's influence on culture through literature, architecture, and the built environment; and *community* — the recovery of human-scaled, civic-minded social order."[10] In the 1920s, "America was already growing twice as fast in the suburbs as in the central cities." At the time, Lewis Mumford and his RPAA colleagues were appalled by the outward expansion intended for New York City, and proposed the decentralization of population into self-sufficient garden cities, an alternative "often mistaken for suburban land subdivisions and landscape gardening," even if RPAA was proposing "complete settlements, not single-use collections of single-family houses."[11] RPAA looked for a solution to the severe shortage of low-cost urban housing and the related problems of slums and overcrowding in America's cities and demonstrated that solid, well-designed homes could be built for working-class people and still provide a return on an investor's capital. The continued occupancy and popularity of the experimental housing developments conceptualized and implemented by the RPAA (e.g., Sunnyside, New York - the first attempt to create a Garden City in America; and Radburn, Fair Lawn, New Jersey), which are now national historic landmarks,[12] demonstrated in time the soundness of RPAA's ideas. In addition, nowadays, many garden city concepts can be seen in the plans and projects of the new urbanists.[13] However, despite the relative success of these early planned communities, they remained isolated experiments unable to dramatically modify the American urban landscape. Especially after WWII, Mumford's discontent with the existing American urban environment continued to grow. In fact, as Bianco (2001) noted, "by the 1950s, he saw the modern American city as all but on the verge of necropolis — the dying city."[14] Mumford's pessimistic view of the American urban environment was reiterated in his 1961 book, *The City in History*:

> In the mass movement into the suburban areas a new kind of community was produced, which caricatured both the historic city and the archetypal suburban refuge: a multitude of uniform, unidentifiable houses, lined up inflexibly, at uniform distances, on uniform roads, in a treeless communal waste, inhabited by people of the same class, the same income, the same age group, witnessing the same television performances, eating the same tasteless prefabricated foods, from the same freezers, conforming in every outward and inward respect to a common mold, manufactured in the central metropolis. Thus the ultimate effect of the suburban escape in our time is, ironically, a low-grade uniform environment from which escape is impossible. (Mumford, 1961:486)

Lewis Mumford's view of the American city was shaped in large part by the evolution of New York, which he closely observed and by the changes implemented in the city by Robert Moses (1888 – 1981), one of the most powerful and controversial public officials of the American scene in the twentieth century. Although for thirty decades Mumford bitterly criticized Moses's endeavors, he admitted, however, that "in the twentieth century, the influence of Robert Moses on the cities of America was greater than that of any other person."[15] Following Moses's death, Golberger noted in a lengthy obituary published in New York Times in July 1981, that for 44 years, from 1924 until 1968, Moses, known as New York's "master builder" (because of the significant amount of infrastructure built under his leadership), directed public works in the city and state and "built parks, highways, bridges, playgrounds, housing, tunnels, beaches, zoos, civic centers, exhibition halls, and the 1964-65 New York World's Fair" valued at $27 billion in 1968 adjusted currency.[16] However, Moses's vision of New York was very different from that embraced at the time by Mumford, and other younger urban planners, such as Jane Jacobs. Moses favored the "open road, the soaring towers, open parks, highways and beaches" and was not concerned with the way the new constructions negatively affected inner-city neighborhood and contributed to an increase in suburban sprawl. (...) When [Moses] left his position as chief of the state park system, the state had 2,567,256 acres. He built 658 playgrounds in New York City, 416 miles of parkways and 13 bridges."[17] Through the works he guided in New York, Moses created an urban model of highways and towers that strongly influenced the planning of cities around the nation. Under his leadership, New York became a "city of mass transit and the nation's first city for the automobile age."[18] Although he never drove a car[19], Moses favored a built urban environment primarily meant to accommodate the automobile. In a 1,246-page carefully researched book (*The Power Broker: Robert Moses and the Fall of New York*) that won the Pulitzer Prize in Biography, Robert Caro (1974), contended that Moses callously removed residents of neighborhoods undergoing urban renewal and had destroyed the traditional fabric of urban neighborhoods in favor of a landscape of red-brick towers.[20] In addition, as one scholar noted,

> Moses remained oblivious to the environmental and political ramifications that his projects would have in the future. Unfettered freeway building displaced thousands, upset political balances and facilitated suburbanization and sprawl, with attendant automobile dependency and environmental degradation Unlike Moses, Lewis Mumford did understand these threats, and his writings expressed fear and anger at the idea of the sort of civilization that was emerging in America. (Bianco, 2001:103)[21]

During his 70-year career, Mumford wrote thousands of pages expressing his views on knowledge, civilization, history, technology, architecture, cities, and the human condition. However, reading his work is not always "easy, soothing, or recreational," as Kenneth Stunkel noted in a recently published book about the key ideas and themes that permeate the voluminous writings of Lewis Mumford.[22] One of this chapter's authors remembers that his first encounter with Mumford's most famous and critically acclaimed book was during an urban theory class he took for the doctorate degree. Completion of Mumford's exhaustive and highly detailed 657 page account of city building since the Neolithic Era was a daunting task, especially since there were three other required books assigned for the course. In light of the struggles to finish the *City in History*, it was interesting to read that some of Mumford's accomplished contemporaries shared the same pain. Ian MacHarg, an influential landscape planner and colleague of Mumford at the University of Pennsylvania, reported that he spent many months attempting to complete this lengthy work after borrowing it from a friend. After he turned the last page with a surge and relief and accomplishment, he laughed out loud when he saw what his friend had written in bold letters at the bottom of the page: "Thank God!"[23] While reading about over 10,000 years of city building history is a feat unto itself, those that have dared to embark on this literary adventure understand why the *City in History* received the prestigious National Book Award and why it sold over 15,000 in the first eight months after publication. Its richness in scholarship and insight make it analogous to the *War and Peace* for city lovers. However, *City in history* (1961)[24] was in fact a revised and expanded version of the *Culture of Cities*[25], a book published in 1938 and considered by many Lewis Mumford's greatest work. A book of great importance in the historical discourse on cities, the *Culture of Cities* must be viewed as part of a larger series that "sought to address the ills of modern life in total by uncovering their root causes in the past and identifying potential courses for their treatment in the present."[26] The framework for the entire series was greatly indebted to Patrick Geddes, a Scottish biologist, sociologist, geographer, philanthropist and pioneering town planner who acted as a mentor to the young Mumford, and who advocated a method of direct observation known as *regional survey*. In preparation for his ambitious series, Mumford carefully examined most of America's major east-coast cities and many Midwestern cities, and during his stay in Europe in 1932, also observed a large variety of the old continent's medieval towns, baroque capitals, and industrial quarters, praising the human scale of medieval towns and the new housing inspired by the British Garden City movement.[27] As Wojtowicz (1999) noted, "what distinguishes the *Culture of Cities* from the other works in the series is Mumford's ability to weave facts and figures, prose and illustrations into an elaborate and evocative carpet that transports the reader to the time and place under examination."[28]

In the *Culture of the Cities*, Mumford also attempts to summarize the course of city development and to correlate this with the rise and fall of civilizations. From a deterministic perspective, the author envisioned a cycle of growth and decay.[29] Strongly influenced by Patrick Geddes when formulating his theories regarding the evolution of cities, Mumford saw city development as passing through six stages/idola: *eopolis* (the village community); *polis* (a protoindustrial city or associated villages); *metropolis* (the mother city; the more mature industrialized city); *megalopolis* (standardizing metropolis; the capitalist city, dominated by bureaucracy, that represents the beginning of the city decline; Paris in the eighteenth century and New York in the early twentieth century would be examples of this stage); *tyrannopolis* (barbarizing megalopolis, dominated by "predatory consumptive parasitism"); and, *necropolis* (the fully decayed and collapsed city).[30] Even if Mumford focused exclusively on urban developments in Western societies,[31] the *City in History* "provides fascinating new material, particularly on prehistoric and ancient sites" and "still has the power to move the present-day reader to dream of a better urban environment, integrated with the surrounding region and attuned to the essential rhythms of daily life."[32]

> This book opens with a city that was, symbolically, a world: it closes with a world that has become, in many practical aspects, a city. In following through this development I have attempted to deal with the forms and functions of the city, and with the purposes that have emerged from it; and I have demonstrated, I trust, that the city will have an even more significant part to play in the future than it has played in the past, if once the original disabilities that have accompanied it through history are sloughed off. (Mumford, 1961: xi)[33]

Mumford begins his epic drama of urban evolution with a description of Paleolithic shrines and burial places, homes of the gods and ancestral spirits where the "first traces of active civic life" are found. "The city of the dead is the forerunner, almost core of every living city." These sanctuaries, cemeteries, and ritual centers served as magnets, drawing nomadic peoples together, like so many pilgrims, in a spirit of awe and reverence."[34] All of these life-enhancing elements-ritual, spiritual communion, family nurture-were carried over into the Neolithic village. Within these prehistoric villages women were planters and food providers were dominant. Mumford idealized these ancient communities, which he viewed as embodying relatively high levels of security, communal cooperation, and face to face intimacy. Work was punctuated by regular rounds of play, conversation, religious ritual, and sexual activity. Rough equality also existed between men and women, since both genders participated in work that was of equal importance. This tranquil village existence gave way to the reemergence of the Paleolithic hunter-chieftain as a deified king within the first cities. Building upon the controversial ideas of the anthropologist Henri Frankfort, Mumford describes the king as the catalytic agent in the first urban implosion. He depicts the demise of the Neolithic village and the rise of urban center in the following manner:

> What actually happened before the city came into existence can only be conjectured. Perhaps residual Paleolithic hunting groups and the new Neolithic settlers, still too sparse to have the upper hand, began to occupy the same territory and stayed together long enough to absorb some of each other's ways and interchange some of their kit of tools. If one dare to call this a marriage of the two cultures, they were probably at first equal partners, but the relationship became increasingly one-sided, as the weapons and coercive habits of the aggressive minority were reinforced by the patient capacity for work that the stone-grinding neolithic peoples showed. As often happens, the rejected component of the earlier culture (hunting) became the new dominant in the agricultural community, but it was now made to do duty for the governance of a superior kind of settlement. Weapons now served not just to kill animals but to threaten and command men. The interplay between the two cultures took place over a long period, but in the end the masculine processes over-rode by sheer dynamism the more passive life-nurturing activities that bore woman's imprint. (Mumford, 1961: 25)

Within the *City in History* Mumford broke from most urban historians of his time by viewing warfare and not international trade as a more important catalyst for city building. Beginning with the ancient Egyptians and Mesopotamians and continuing into his own time, Mumford purported that nations were just as likely to "conquer and destroy foreign markets" as they were willing to engage in active trade with them. Whether it was a deified ruler in ancient Egypt, a fascist dictator in 20th Century Germany, or even a democratically elected leader of the American empire, Mumford provides detailed examples of how every earthly empire erects monumental architecture to strike "respectful terror" in the hearts of the outsider, as well as the citizen.[35]

Two exceptions Mumford noted in his observations of thousands of years of urban development were the Greek polis and the medieval town. In the Aegean Sea between the eighth and sixth centuries B.C. there was "devolution of power from the citadel to the democratic, village-based community." The Greeks' village ways made them distrustful of kingly power and centralized rule. Subsequently, they demythologized their leaders and made them dependent upon popular support and a common constitution. Even their gods acted more like mortals than the divine creatures worshipped by the ancient Egyptians or modern day Christians or Muslims. Like the humans who made sacrifices to them, the Greek gods were susceptible to the same amorous drives and jealous rivalries as those they supposedly ruled over. Athens, the queen city of ancient Greece, was not impressive architecturally, but as with any great city, "the life it contained was more significant than the container." This was a civilization presided over by gifted amateurs contemptuous of specialists and mousy administrators. It was the generalist whom the Greeks, and Lewis Mumford, most admired. As an astute scholar of these "all-rounders," Mumford understood Aristotle's comment that a gentleman should be able to pay the flute, but not too well.[36]

In the Hellenic polis the "rich and the poor were side by side" and "the physician received the same rate of pay as the craftsman." In tandem with this equalitarian lifestyle the Greeks embraced, affluent citizens were more likely to spend their money in the construction of temples and statues than on private homes. Mumford observed that the Romans at the height of their empire took a dramatic break from Greek equalitarianism, as wealthy Romans often felt compelled to own extravagant homes in both Rome and the countryside. The materialism and conspicuous consumption of the ancient Romans gave way to equally dramatic changes in urban planning. While most streets in both Athens and Sparta were at best narrow and twisted walkways for small groups of people, Roman boulevards were built wide enough to sustain massive armies and subsequent military parades. Civilization would have to wait a few hundred years for the return of the "urbane village," in areas such as Chipping Camden and Burford in England. Mumford viewed the "widening in the center for a marketplace" and "row houses set on long narrow lots" and "not mechanically stamped out," as embodying some of the best urban development practices within Europe. The author praised the late medieval planning style that adroitly combined urbanity with openness.[37] In Mumford's view the medieval city serves as the basis for the *ideal city*. According to Mumford, the modern city resembles the Roman city (the sprawling megalopolis), which ended in collapse and risks to share the same fate if significant changes in the planning of urban communities are not made.[38]

Throughout The City in History Mumford plays the role of a perpetual critic of the "urban devastation" in the form of "multiple lane expressways which "often cut through the city core." The author prophetically viewed American's obsession with the automobile as leading to the ultimate destruction of the country's best urbane villages, such as Georgetown, Washington D.C. and Greenwich Village, the large residential neighborhood on the west side of Lower Manhattan in New York City. The cities Mumford favored were well-proportioned with compact civic centers and vivid neighborhood life. The village in the city is his ideal community. Nowhere is this more apparent than in Mumford's description of Cambridge, Massachusetts. He described this idyllic

American urban center as possessing "the intimate charm of the village" coupled with "the sophisticated dash of a metropolis"[39]

One of his "radical" ideas for mitigating the leveling of urban neighborhoods for parking lots and expressways was to require motorists to park their vehicles on the outskirts of the city and subsequently rely on public transportation to work or play in the urban core. While residents of large metropolitan areas such as Washington D.C., London, U.K., or even Chicago know that often the most efficient (and cost effective) way of navigating these cities is via the subway. In addition, many American cities have found success in closing off certain tourist attraction streets to car traffic. Beale Street in Memphis, Bourbon Street in New Orleans, and 4th Street in Louisville are examples of pedestrian only districts which continue to grow in popularity. Mumford aptly observed that even car obsessed Americans may find attractive unique neighborhoods within metropolitan areas. As the author noted with "all the monuments of Washington D.C., we [still] want to spend most of our time walking around Georgetown."[40] This feeling might be presently shared by numerous people and might explain why many Americans are now leaving (or have left) their low density suburbs to return to their local "Georgetowns" within historical neighborhoods or why they relocate to new urbanism communities on the city's edge.

Favorite Cities: Venice and Amsterdam

In light of Mumford's affinity for cities favoring pedestrians and public transportation over the expressway-dominated metropolis, it is not surprising that he praised Venice, the charming Italian city. An urban creation founded by a group of refugees fleeing the Huns, the first Venetians drained marshes and dredged canals along the shallow waters of the Adriatic to build their utopian city. The gondola (mentioned as early as 1094) was "the perfect technical adaptation to these narrow, shallow waterways." Anyone who has visited Venice knows that these flat bottomed boats and a few of their motorized cousins are more than just a tourist attraction; they consist of the only way to traverse the city outside of walking, since cars are not allowed within city limits. Mumford admired the Venetians' ability to transform a previously uninhabitable marsh environment into a bustling mercantile city and praised Venice's "functional zoning" that took the form of greater and lesser islands disposed around the central city, contending that a handicap has been turned into an opportunity.[41] Mumford favored this type of "organic" planning where urban development complements, instead of destroying or polluting, land and seascapes. Organic development is combined with a decentralized planning strategy in Venice, where Piazza San Marco, the main plaza along the Grand Canal and home to San Marco's Cathedral, is repeated on a smaller scale in each of the city's parishes. Each parish, often in the shape of a trapezoid, includes a fountain, a church, and a school. The approximately 200 canals in Venice serve as both boundaries and connecting links for each neighborhood; "they are both watersheds and arterial highways, functioning like the greenbelts and through motorways of a well-designed modern town, though not so reckless an urban space as American highways or the neighborhood greenbelts of English New Towns."[42] Essentially, Mumford heralded Venice for being able to adapt to change and growth through organic planning and decentralization "with a unified but varied traffic system, with canals that preserved openness, with comely row houses and gardens, and continuous tree-lined arcades." In Mumford's view, Amsterdam "rivaled Versailles in beauty without sacrifice of utility."[43] As Mumford noted, Amsterdam, the lively mercantile northern European city, absorbed "all the commercial lessons the Italians could teach."[44] The author also observed that Amsterdam was one of the first European cities to balance capitalism with governmental regulation through a series of building ordinances. As in Venice, a substantial amount of public control was necessary in Amsterdam in order to both reclaim and protect land within this below-sea-level city. In the end, a skillful mixture of free market opportunities and public regulations produced a metropolitan area that is almost as vibrant today as it was in the 1500s. Nowadays, it is probably fair to say that Amsterdam's economic greatness has surpassed that of its mentor city; while contemporary Venice is almost completely reliant on tourism for sustainability, Amsterdam embodies a more diverse economic base. Holland's canal city has been able to foster a progressive and innovative economy while maintaining (for the most part) a decentralized planning model reminiscent of Venice.

Lasting Influences

While it is true that Mumford expressed many times a pessimistic view regarding the evolution of the city, the author recognized the limitations of his research and also foresaw a solution to the urban decay he observed in America and elsewhere.

> Social life has its own laws and rhythms; much remains hidden or irrational; much escapes empiric observation and still more escapes statistical analysis. All one can say with any surety is this: when a city has reached the megalopolitan stage, it is plainly on the downward path: it needs a terrific exertion of social force to overcome the inertia, to alter the direction of movement, to resist the immanent processes of disintegration. (...) But while there is life, there is the possibility of counter-movement [and] fresh growth. (Mumford quoted in Dorman, 1993: 228)[45]

In Mumford's view, the potential stage in the city cyclic evolution that could emerge from a declining phase of any city is the "ecological or organic *idolum*," which represents Mumford's urban ideal.[46]

> We need a new image of order, which shall include the organic and personal, and eventually embrace all the offices and functions of

> man. Only if we can project that image shall we be able to find a new
> form for the city. (Mumford, 1961: 4)

As an alternative to the sprawling of American suburbs of the post-World War II era that seemed to Mumford to "lack any sense of communal focus with their separate residential, commercial and cultural centers and their emphasis on automobile transportation" Mumford proposed "the establishment of moderately dense regional cities to siphon off some of the pressure on American metropolitan areas."[47] And Mumford's "*organic idolum*," which "consists of neighborhoods, small towns, agricultural areas, small cities, the use of a river valley region as the primary unit of planning analysis, moderate-density communities, emphasis on human-scale garden cities as centers for new growth, creation of economies balanced between capitalist and socialist models, revival of historic parts of cities, new, smaller, human-scale technology" became at the end of the twentieth century the ideal of neo-traditional urban planners.[48] In particular, as Bianco contended, the New Urbanists' ideas influenced by Mumford's vision of the organic city are: "mixed-use design, allowing for a combination of land uses (residential, commercial, services); compact, human-scale architecture and street design (narrow streets, back alleys, sidewalks, smaller buildings); central common areas (plazas and parks); planned greenbelts between urbanized areas and greenspaces within; pedestrian- and transit-orientated design; medium to high densities (as opposed to low-density sprawl); limits on urban growth (through the Urban Growth Boundary); greater reliance on alternative modes of transportation (walking, bicycling, mass transit, etc.)."[49]

However, as Lind (1999) observed, "Mumford, who like many early-twentieth-century architecture critics was concerned with housing for low-income workers, would have warned that the New Urbanism will be a failure if its only lasting products are ghettoes for the affluent like Seaside, Florida, and Disney's Celebration."[50] Reservations toward some early new urbanist communities have been expressed by Wojtowicz (the literary executor for the Mumford Estate) as well. The author noted that "the recent spate of neo-traditional suburbs — including Seaside, Florida and Kentlands, Maryland — would have ultimately dissatisfied Mumford. Though they imitate the pedestrian scale and Romantic architecture of older American towns, they do not provide the unique civic focal points, let alone the civic institutions, that have defined all great cities from ancient Athens to Renaissance Florence."[51]

Nevertheless, if Moses's low density, automobile dominated model for urban development set the trend for planning in the 20th Century, Mumford's influences may well set the trend for urban development in the 21st Century. Mumford favored decentralization, but not suburban sprawl and was one of the first who considered dangerous for the long-term health of the city the prioritization of the needs of the car in urban planning decisions. And this observation is one that resonates strongly nowadays. Currently, no rational elected public official is calling for the expansion of expressways or interstates which were at the core of virtually every development plan proposed during the post-Cold War Era. In our post housing and credit bubble world, sustainable development is more important than massive development. Mumford may have been a lone critic of Moses' blitzkrieg-like destruction of older and often historically significant neighborhoods within New York to make way for his construction schemes, but today such proposals are often fiercely countered by inner-city dwellers who consider them undemocratic, governmentally intrusive, and unjust. In addition, in light of the plus-trillion-dollar federal deficit our nation is facing, this type of infrastructure projects is not only cost prohibitive, but also politically unfeasible. Recent history suggests that Mumford's urbane village won more fans than Moses' six lane expressways.

For instance, if in the years that followed WWII, Mumford's proposals regarding Portland's growth (e.g., emphasis on regionalism and population dispersal to new satellite towns) were dismissed in favor of Moses's ideas, "a shift in political culture in the 1960s and 1970s, (...) brought a renewed commitment to the ideals Mumford had espoused and, today, the Portland area's regional planning agency, Metro, has adopted a Regional Framework Plan that embraces the Mumfordian vision, with an almost blatant rejection of Moses' commitment to freeways, bridges and other types of massive investment in auto-accommodating infrastructure."[52]

Mumford spoke out "in favor of historic preservation before it became fashionable and opposed urban planners who demolished human-scale neighborhoods to create monstrous highways and housing projects."[53] Currently, the influence of his ideas is evidenced by the substantial growth in historical preservation districts in cities such as Boston, Louisville, and even Los Angeles, and also within new growth areas - America's suburbs. Mayors such as Jim Brainard of Carmel, located just outside of Indianapolis, have shaped retail and residential development plans around many of Mumford's proposals. [54] Mumford, the National Book Award winner would feel right at home in this Midwestern suburb with high density neighborhoods featuring traditional architecture, expansion in number of bike paths, walking paths, and green spaces, as well as the restoration and growth of the old downtown area. Carmel may be one of the most politically conservative communities in the country, but its city officials and many of its residents have wholeheartedly embraced the neighborhood ideals of the man deemed "an outspoken revolutionary" by Robert Moses.[55]

Mumford contended that "the city should be a man's greatest work of art"[56] and his skill in observing and describing how some cities mastered the art of urban design, while many others failed to do so, is a gift that continues to grace many of America's most innovative and resourceful communities.

Notes

1. R. Wojtowicz, City As Community: The Life And Vision of Lewis Mumford, *Quest*, January 2001, Volume 4 (1), pp.1-4.

2. R. Wojtowicz, City As Community: The Life And Vision of Lewis Mumford, *Quest*, January 2001, Volume 4 (1), pp.1-4.

3. See D. L. Miller, *Lewis Mumford: A Life*, (New York: Weidenfeld & Nicolson, 1989).

4. Ibid.

5. Lewis Mumford was the leading spokesman and theoretician for the RPAA. Mumford also introduced RPAA members to the ideas of Patrick Geddes, a proponent of Ebenezer Howard and his Garden City idea, a concept eventually embraced by RPAA.

6. E. Talen, Beyond the Front Porch: Regionalist Ideals in the New Urbanist Movement, *Journal of Planning History* 2008 vol. 7(1), pp. 20-47, p. 20.

7. See Sunnyside Gardens Historic District Designation Report (New York City Landmarks Preservation Commission, June 26, 2007; http://www.landmarkwatch.org/PDF/2SunnysideGardens.pdf).

8. K.C. Parsons, Collaborative Genius: The Regional Planning Association of America, *Journal of the American Planning Association*, 1994, 60(4): 462-482.

9. M. Luccarelli, *Lewis Mumford and the Ecological Region: The Politics of Planning* (New York, NY: The Guilford Press, 1995, pp.3-4).

10. Luccarelli, *op. cit.*, p. 22.

11. E. Talen, *New Urbanism and American Planning: The Conflict of Cultures*, (New York: Routledge, 2005, pp. 3-4).

12. The Sunnyside Gardens Historic District has been declared a New York City Landmark on October 2007, after a four year process. It was listed on the National Register of Historic Places in 1984. Although Radburn was never fully built because of the onset of Depression, the community's original goals have been achieved and the built areas continued to be very popular. In 2005, Radburn was designated a National Historical Landmark. For additional information about the other mid-20th century garden cities built by Clarence Stein and his colleagues, which achieved historic distinction, see http://www.landmarkwatch.org/gardenCity.html.

13. See K. C. Parsons and D. Schuyler, eds., *From Garden City to Green City: The Legacy of Ebenezer Howard*, (Baltimore: The Johns Hopkins University Press, 2002).

14. M. J. Bianco, Robert Moses and Lewis Mumford: Competing Paradigms of Growth in Portland, Oregon. *Planning Perspectives,* 2001, p. 104.

15. Mumford quoted in R. Caro, The *Power Broker: Robert Moses and the Fall of New York (*New York: Alfred A. Knopf, 1974, p. 12).

16. P. Goldberger, Robert Moses, Master Builder, is Dead at 92. New York Times, July 30, 1981. http://www.nytimes.com/learning/general/onthisday/bday/1218.html.

17. Ibid.

18. Ibid.

19. R. A. Caro, The *Power Broker: Robert Moses and the Fall of New York,* (New York: Alfred A. Knopf, 1974).

20. Ibid.

21. M. J. Bianco, Robert Moses and Lewis Mumford: Competing Paradigms of Growth in Portland, Oregon. *Planning Perspectives,* 2001, 16: 95–114.

22. K.R. Stunkel, *Understanding Lewis Mumford: A Guide for the Perplexed*, (Lewiston, N.Y.: The Edwin Mellon Press, 2004:7).

23. D. L. Miller, *Lewis Mumford: A Life,* (New York: Weidenfeld & Nicolson, 1989).

24. L. Mumford, *The City in History,* (New York: Harvest Books, 1961).

25. L. Mumford, *The Culture of Cities* (New York: Harcourt, Brace and Company, 1938).

26. R. Wojtowicz. Review of Mumford, Lewis, *The Culture of Cities*. H-Urban, H-Net Reviews. January, 1999. URL: http://www.h-net.org/reviews/showrev.php?id=266.

27. Ibid.

28. Ibid.

29. R. L. Dorman, *Revolt of the Provinces: The Regionalist Movement in America 1920-1945* (University of North Carolina Press, 1993, p. 227).

30. Bianco, *op. cit.*, p. 104.

31. In the preface of his book *The City in History*, Mumford (1961: xi) noted that in all his studies of the city he relied on experience and direct observation, a method of inquiry that books cannot replace. As a result, his discourse was limited to the Western civilization and even there, as the author admitted, he had "to leave out large significant tracts: namely, Spain and Latin America, Palestine, Eastern Europe, Soviet Russia."

32. Robert Wojtowicz. Review of Mumford, Lewis, *The Culture of Cities*. H-Urban, H-Net Reviews. January, 1999. URL: http://www.h-net.org/reviews/showrev.php?id =266.

33. Mumford, 1961.

34. Ibid.

35. Ibid.

36. Miller, *op. cit.*

37. Mumford, 1961.

38. Wojtowicz, 2001.

39. Mumford, *op.cit., 1961.*

40. Mumford, *op.cit.*

41. Mumford, *op.cit.*

42. Mumford, *op.cit.*

43. Mumford, *op.cit.*

44. Mumford, *op.cit.*

45. Dorman, *op. cit.*

46. Bianco, *op. cit.*, p. 104.

47. Wojtowicz, 2001.

48. Bianco, *op. cit.*, p. 104.

49. Ibid.

50. M. Lind, Urban Philosopher: A Walking Tour of Lewis Mumford, December 30, 1999, New America Foundation, http://newamerica.net/node/5660.

51. Wojtowicz, 2001, p.4.

52. Bianco, 2001, p. 95.

53. M. Lind, 1999.

54. Mayor Jim Brainard, interview by Karl Besel, 2009.

55. Moses quoted in R. Caro, 1974, p. 471.

56. Mumford quoted in Dorman, 1993, p. 228.

Chapter Two

Lewis Mumford and Jane Jacobs as Precursors of New Urbanism: Residents' Reaction to Different Urban Visions

Viviana Andreescu and Karl Besel

Lewis Mumford, a social philosopher, architecture critic, and historian and Jane Jacobs, a "geographer, propagandist, and city planning idealist"[1] were two writers whose keen eyes for urban details and reformist ideas about urban planning and architecture strongly influenced the way we perceive urban forms today or think about the future of our cities. However, as Goldberger noted, "Mumford loved theories as much as Jacobs hated them, and he thought that the city could be made rational. Jacobs knew better. It was the very randomness of things that she loved — she took solace from the unpredictability and messiness of the city while Mumford sought only to bring more order to it."[2]

Nonetheless, although their perspectives regarding the urban space diverged in many respects, Mumford and Jacobs are both considered precursors of the New Urbanism and they both contributed different ideas that informed many of the guiding principles of the neo-traditional planning and design movement (i.e., walkability; connectivity; mixed-use and diversity; mixed-housing; quality architecture and urban design; traditional neighborhood structures; increased density; green transportation; sustainability; quality of life).

This chapter intends to briefly present comparatively some of Jacobs's and Mumford's views of the city and planning proposals. In addition, our intention was to observe how the American public responded to these alternative perspectives of the city life. Taking into account the fact that the ultimate goal of Mumford's and Jacobs's prescriptions was to obtain an improved quality of urban life — an objective shared by the new urbanists as well — we examined one aspect of the quality of life in a large American city (i.e., residential satisfaction) and tried to determine which factors were more likely to influence public perceptions of urban neighborhoods at the beginning of the 21st century, a period when new urbanism reached prominence in the United States[3].

Two Different Perspectives of the Urban Environment: Jane Jacobs and Lewis Mumford

Jane Jacobs (1916-2006) published in 1961 a manuscript *(The Death and Life of Great American Cities)*[4] that some critics[5] consider the 20th-century most influential book about cities, which helped "shift many urbanites' understanding and treatment of their cities."[6] According to Palen,[7] as a result of Jane Jacobs's influence "the planners of today are far more conscious of the social impact of design and planning decisions" and "the message that cities are for people is finally affecting urban policies."As Paul Goldberger, a Pulitzer Prize-winning architect critic noted, "Jacobs was not a professional planner, and an ongoing theme of her life and work was the deep conflict she felt about the relationship of knowledge to professional expertise."[8] Nevertheless, Jane Jacobs's book *The Death and Life of Great American Cities* managed to challenge orthodox city planning in the postwar era and is considered nowadays a touchstone and a source of inspiration for many urban planners, architects, and other professionals concerned with city life.

Like Lewis Mumford's book *The City in History*[9], Jane Jacobs's book, "a 457-page polemic against traditional planning"[10] was printed at the beginning of a decade that had to face a revival of the metropolitan crisis. Within a generation after the Second World War, the optimistic atmosphere that encouraged in the United States the mid-twentieth-century urban renaissance almost disappeared and by the end of the 1960s the ills of the great cities had become a national obsession.[11] Jacobs's work emerged from the big-city milieu of the 1950s: its politics, social life, and architecture. The Housing Acts of 1947 and 1954, the national Urban Renewal Act of 1948, the Interstate Highways Act of 1956, large slum clearances, the construction of federally financed low-income multistoried apartment buildings, recent usages of urban renewal land for upper-middle class housing or for institutional purposes, the growth of suburbs, the impact of the automobile, etc. were real social and physical developments of the mid-twentieth-century urban America, Jacobs was aware of.[12] In Jane Jacobs's view, "the network of small-scale, local communities within larger, heterogeneous cities — a pattern she first saw in New York in the 1950s and which for her had always been the source of both urban and societal health — was breaking down, unable to be sustained in the sprawling world of automobiles and technology in which we live."[13]

According to Peter Dreier, Jane Jacobs was "a public intellectual, who put her ideas into practice."She had a profound influence on city planning but also on community activism in United States and later in Canada, where she moved in 1968. Although their views regarding a livable city were different, Jane Jacobs and Lewis Mumford both profoundly disliked Robert Moses's urban renewal strategies. When Moses, "New York's planning czar and perhaps the most powerful unelected city official of the 20th century, "proposed building a highway bisecting the Greenwich Village neighborhood, Jane Jacobs became fully engaged in the battle to save her community and managed to catalyze a broader grassroots movement that contributed to the 1969 cancellation of Moses's expressway plan in New York and made mayors and planning agencies in other US cities to reconsider the "bulldozer approach to urban renaissance." The urban renewal program was eventually canceled by President Nixon in 1974.[14]

While not an "advocate planner,"[15] Jane Jacobs opposed conventional urban redevelopment planning favoring diversity of uses, small scale development, and preservation of the character of the old neighborhoods. A central theme in her book is that the character of the physical environment has fundamental, direct effects on a city's social life, especially at the neighborhood level. Jacobs considered that neighborhoods could play a major role in maintaining a sense of community and safety within the larger city. In Jacobs's view, the communities of planners, with their high-rise apartments, limited lines of movement, and excessive open spaces, inherently led to a lack of neighborliness and a breakdown of a natural system of order.[16]

> To approach a city, or even a city neighborhood as if it were large architectural problem, capable of being given order by converting it into a disciplined work of art, is to make the mistake of attempting to substitute art for life. (Jacobs, 1961:373)[17]

Jane Jacobs considered that a mix of social activities and a heterogeneous population would increase a neighborhood's vitality. By advocating mixed populations and land usages she directly challenged one of the basic tenets of city planning.[18] The urban planners, architects, and reformers who imported ideas from Ebenezer Howard, the founder of New Towns, "Garden City" movement in England and were advocating greenbelts, low densities, and separate zones for different activities were highly criticized by Jane Jacobs. She argued that "the problem of insecurity cannot be solved by spreading people out more thinly, trading the characteristics of cities for the characteristics of suburbs."[19]

Jacobs also attacked Le Corbusier's "radiant city" model and rejected the idea of large-scale city planning. Jacobs's path model toward an ideal city might be briefly described as a combination of diversity, vitality, and safety. The author acknowledged that "if we are to maintain a city society that can diagnose and keep abreast of deeper social problems, the starting point must be, in any case, to strengthen whatever workable forces for maintaining safety and civilization in the cities we do have."[20]

Jacobs's book evoked different types of reactions. While some critics considered her attempt a fresh and challenging approach to urban policy, others dismissed her arguments as trivial.[21] One author, for instance, contended that...

> Jane Jacobs' spirited defense of traditional neighborhoods shares all the unrealities that mar F.J. Osborn's defense of Howard's vision. The neighborhood world is dying (...). Doubtless enclaves of neighborhood life will continue to exist, but they will remain merely enclaves - in contemporary society the counterpart of the existing medieval and Renaissance towns that attract the tourist to Europe for visual respite from the urban monotony that is rapidly prevailing in the most cities of the world. Modern city planning offers no solution to this dismal tendency, for it presupposes the very social factors that are producing the present urban blight.[22]

Additionally, some reviewers noted that Jacobs's preoccupation with street safety made her oblivious to other urban problems and values. Palen, for example, contended that in Jacobs's view characteristics of the urban scene such as convenience, beauty, the absence of the noise of trucks crowding the street, or low pollution levels are less important than safety.[23] Choldin however, observed that even if the effects on life in the city of some major social events that were under way (e.g., the mass migration of blacks from the rural South or the baby boom) were not mentioned in her book, Jacobs anticipated one social development which was about to happen — the urban explosion of crime and fear.[24]

Nonetheless, from a different theoretical perspective, Lewis Mumford did not think that Jacobs's suggestions for improvement of the city life were more than simple "home remedies for urban cancer"[25] and argued that there are other and better ways than Jacobs's to reorder the twentieth-century urban environment in the United States. Mumford did not perceive the metropolitan civilization as a success and labeled it "a different kind of wilderness" where "the feral rather than the humane quality [was] dominant." More than three decades before Jacobs's book was published, Mumford contended that "the cities of America must learn to remold our mechanical and financial regime; for if metropolitanism continues, they are probably destined to fall by its weight."[26] Without addressing the socio-economic considerations that produced slums, decay and poverty in the city and placing more emphasis on the aesthetic rather than the social side of planning, "the programs, policies, and plans of the early metropolitan period of American Urban history had shown little promise of providing the humane metropolitan society that Mumford had hoped for."[27]

As a leader in the Regional Planning Association of America, an informal group of planners, architects, social theorists, and housing experts, Mumford, was among those highly criticized by Jacobs, who supported the "physical design" tradition in the United States, considering it the appropriate way of developing more reasonable and more livable urban communities. Like Ebenezer Howard, Mumford was a proponent of the peripheral planned community and believed that the existing city world would fail. Jane Jacobs and William Whyte on the other hand believed in the existing city and considered planned communities anti-urban.[28]

In a review of *Garden Cities of Tomorrow* published in the New York Review of Books and dated April 8, 1965, Mumford, who once considered Jacobs his disciple, wrote: "…Jane Jacobs' preposterous mass of historic misinformation and contemporary misinterpretation in her *The Life and Death of Great American Cities* exposed her ignorance of the whole planning movement."[29] Although Mumford recognized the universality of the bad fashionable urban patterns described by Jacobs in her 1961 book, the author stated that Jacobs's "new costume of theory exposes large areas of naked unawareness," which undermine her statements. In addition, Mumford contended that "some of [Jacobs's] boldest planning proposals, rest on faulty data, inadequate evidence, and startling miscomprehensions of views contrary to hers."[30] As a supporter of Howard's and Le Corbusier's ideas, Mumford also noted that "obviously, neither radiance (sunlight), nor gardens, nor spaciousness, nor beauty can have any place in Mrs.

Jacobs' picture of a great city."[31] Referring to Jane Jacobs's "original theory," "new principles of town planning," or "ultimate criteria of sound metropolitan planning" (i.e., dynamism, density, and diversity), Mumford, observed that London of the 18th century or contemporary Harlem with its high density, pedestrian filled streets, crosslines of circulation, and a mixture of primary economic activities met Jacobs's *ideal* conditions without achieving the favorable results Jacobs expected in her prescriptions.[32]

Mumford[33] also contended that Jacobs emphasized the necessity for continued street life because "her ideal city was mainly an organization for the prevention of crime."In response to Jacobs's affirmations that "there is a basic aesthetic limitation on what can be done with cities" and "a city cannot be a work of art,"[34] Mumford underlined some of the basic elements of his theoretical perspective and listed the desirable characteristics of a great city:

> It is the beauty of great urban cathedrals and palaces, the order of great monastic structures or the university precincts of Oxford and Cambridge, the serenity and spaciousness of the great squares of Paris, London, Rome, Edinburgh, that have preserved intact the urban cores of truly great cities over many centuries. (...) Beauty, order, spaciousness, clarity of purpose may be worth having for their direct effect on the human spirit even if they do not promote dynamism, increase the turnover of goods, or reduce criminal violence.[35]

Comparing Jacobs's and Mumford's views of the city, Talen stressed the essential contrast between these two perspectives and also observed that American settlements fall short of either's perspective's main objective — a revitalized core or a clustered and coherently settled region.[36]

Factors Influencing the Residents' Perceptions of the Urban Environment

Based on their personal experiences, observation, historical facts, and scholarly research, Jacobs and Mumford tried to present the elements that would characterize in an objective way a good, livable city. However, when formulating their vision of the ideal city, none of the two authors seemed to have relied on data measuring the inhabitants' subjective perceptions of the urban environment, considering them a priori known truths. Using data collected from a probability sample of residents of a large American city, our intention is to estimate to what extent Jacobs's and Mumford's perceptions of the Americans' spatial environmental preferences could be considered valid in our time. Even if the empirical base required to identify determinants of community satisfaction is larger than the selected set of indicators included in the present analysis, certain preliminary inferences regarding the authenticity of Jane Jacobs' and Lewis Mumford's assumptions and predictions will be made, as supported by statistical evidence.

Based on Jacobs's arguments, it would be expected that people who feel safe and secure in their urban environment, who feel they are part of their neighborhoods, who trust their neighbors, and are satisfied with the way people watch for the others' goods in one's neighborhood would also express a higher level of satisfaction toward their urban community.   Based   on   Mumford's assumptions, we would hypothesize that people who are satisfied with their neighborhood's appearance, degree of cleanliness, amount of peace and quiet, and of open space would express a significantly higher level of neighborhood satisfaction than those dissatisfied with these particular aspects of their urban environment.

The source of the data is a telephone survey carried out in 2001by a research team from the Department of Sociology, University of Louisville, Louisville, KY. A random sample of 421 individuals was designed to ensure maximum representativity for the adult population of the city of Louisville. Data have been analyzed by means of logistic regression, an objective, multivariate statistical procedure able to estimate the probability of an event occurring. The main objective of this analysis is to establish which variables included in the model better predict neighborhood satisfaction in a specific urban setting. Results have been presented for the overall sample and separately for homeowners and renters. Taking into account the fact that the analysis will refer to only one urban setting (Louisville),[37] that might not be regarded as a typical *great American city*, and considering that this is a secondary analysis (e.g., only a limited number of predictors were available to be included in the model; relative small sample size), the results should be regarded as tentative.

It should be noted that 86.2% of the respondents who have been interviewed declared they were satisfied with their neighborhood. Satisfaction with the city of Louisville was expressed by the large majority (94.1%) of respondents as well. The analysis presented here examines the effect on *neighborhood satisfaction* (a dummy variable coded 1 for respondents who declared they were satisfied and very satisfied with their neighborhood and zero otherwise) of four main predictors (perceived safety, neighborliness, neighborhood general appearance, and the amount of open space) and includes two control variables (homeownership and race).

Perceived safety is a composite measure that includes responses at four questions (i.e., 1. Are you afraid of being attacked, when walking at night in the neighborhood? 2. Are you afraid of leaving personal property outside unattended? 3. Are you afraid of leaving doors unlocked? 4. Are you afraid about someone breaking into the home to steal things?). All variables were recoded and transformed into dummy variables (coded 1 for lack of fear of crime and zero otherwise) prior to the factorial analysis that has been used to construct this indicator. Only one factor was extracted when Principal Component Analysis (PCA) was used (Eigenvalue = 2.007; % variance explained = 50.173; factor loadings varied from .629 to .758). The reliability coefficient Alpha = .666.

Neighborliness is also a composite measure constructed through factor analysis. Respondents were asked to evaluate their level of satisfaction with: (1) the way people in their neighborhood watch out for the others' goods; (2) the extent to which people in their neighborhood can be trusted; (3) feels he/she is part of the neighborhood. When PCA was performed only one factor was extracted (Eigenvalue = 1.940; % variance explained = 64.659; factor loadings varied from .739 to .845) and reliability coefficient Alpha for this variable was .726.

Neighborhood appearance is a composite measure that estimated the respondent's level of satisfaction with: (1) the neighborhood general appearance; (2) the way people keep litter picked up; (3) amount of peace and quiet in the neighborhood. The variable was also created through factorial analysis and one factor was extracted (Eigenvalue = 1.850; % variance explained =61.50; factor loadings varied from .711 to .820). The reliability coefficient Alpha = .685. The analysis also included a variable that measured the respondents' level of satisfaction with the amount of *open space* existing in their neighborhood. This is a dummy variable, coded 1 for those who were satisfied and zero otherwise. *Homeownership* was a dummy variable coded 1 for homeowners and zero otherwise. *Race* was also a dummy variable (coded 1 for white respondents and zero for others). Table 2.1 presents the results of the logistic regression for the overall sample and for two subsamples (homeowners and renters).

Table 2.1: Logit Estimates for Neighborhood Satisfaction

Variables	Overall sample (N=421)		Homeowners (N=259)		Renters (N=162)	
	B (SE)	Odds Ratio	B (SE)	Odds Ratio	B (SE)	Odds Ratio
Neighborhood safety level	.800** (.275)	2.225	.492 (.336)	1.636	1.290** (.494)	3.632
Satisfaction with neighbors	.352* (.181)	1.421	.511 (.268)	1.666	.185 (.252)	1.203
Neighborhood appearance	.855*** (.180)	2.352	.800*** (.239)	2.226	.970*** (.291)	2.639
Amount of open space	.974** (.364)	2.648	1.036* (.491)	2.819	.966 (.562)	2.527
Homeownership	-.536 (.404)	.585				
Race (White)	-.041 (.389)	.960	.166 (.545)	1.181	-.307 (.561)	.736
Constant	2.432*** (.531)	11.38	1.582** (.569)	4.864	2.906*** (.789)	18.28
Pseudo R² (Nagelkerke)	.447		.385		.515	

Goodness-of-Fit	χ^2	p	χ^2	p	χ^2	p
	7.138	.522	6.443	.598	7.258	.509

* p≤.05, **p≤.01, ***p≤.001 (2-tail test)

It can be observed that in the overall sample (N =421), those who feel safe in their neighborhood are more likely to express neighborhood satisfaction. Although the level of one's satisfaction with his/her neighbors is positively associated with neighborhood satisfaction, the relationship is not strong enough to be statistically significant. The variables that contribute the most to the model are satisfaction with the neighborhood general appearance and satisfaction with the amount of open space. Specifically, given that the other variables in the model are held constant, the odds for persons who are satisfied with the amount of open space to be also satisfied with their neighborhood are more than twice larger (OR = 2.648) than the odds for the persons who are not satisfied with the amount of open space. Homeownership status and race are not significantly related to the neighborhood satisfaction. Although in the overall sample homeowners and white respondents appear to be less satisfied with their neighborhoods than, respectively, renters and racial minorities differences in attitudes are not very large. Approximately 45% (Nagelkerke Pseudo R^2 = .447) of the variation in neighborhood satisfaction is explained by the variables included in this overall model.

The additional statistical models included in Table 2.1 examine the relationships between the selected predictors and neighborhood satisfaction for two subsamples — homeowners and those who do not own the house they live in. It can be noticed that the selected variables seem to explain better variations in neighborhood satisfaction for the subsample of renters (Nagelkerke Pseudo R^2 = .515) compared to the subsample of owners (Nagelkerke Pseudo R^2 = .385). In addition, the analysis indicates that the selected predictors have differential effects on neighborhood satisfaction when homeownership status is held constant. In particular, it can be observed that the level of fear of crime impacts significantly a person's level of satisfaction with his/her neighborhood only if he/she is a renter.

Although the variable neighborliness (or satisfaction with neighbors) is not statistically significant in any of the two subsamples, it has a significant and positive impact on neighborhood satisfaction in the overall sample. This and the direction of the effect suggest that homeowners and renters seem to be more satisfied with their neighborhoods if they trust their neighbors, know they can rely on them for watching their goods, or feel a part of their neighborhood. For both subsamples, satisfaction with the general appearance of the neighborhood predicts neighborhood satisfaction. If for renters satisfaction with the amount of open space does not significantly influence attitudes, for homeowners it does. Specifically, the odds of being satisfied with one's neighborhood increase by a factor of 2.819 for homeowners who are satisfied with the amount of open space compared to homeowners who do not think there is sufficient open space in their neighborhood. Although race is not significant in any of the models presented here, it can be observed that while non-minority homeowners tend to be more satisfied with their neighborhoods than minority homeowners, non-minority renters are less satisfied with their neighborhoods than minority renters.

Discussing the research findings

The analysis presented here tried to identify some of the factors more likely to predict neighborhood satisfaction in a large American city. The selection of the variables we used in the statistical analyses presented in this chapter was based on Jacobs's and Mumford's descriptions of desirable urban spaces. Based on Jacobs's predictions, we anticipated that fear of crime and concerns with safety would have a significant impact in structuring individual perceptions of the urban environment. The data used in this study show, however, that the level of neighborhood satisfaction expressed by Louisvillians did not appear to be equally influenced by these factors. Although perceived safety is positively associated with Louisville's homeowners' residential satisfaction, the effect is not sufficiently strong to be significant, suggesting that there are other characteristics of the place that may have a stronger impact on homeowners' residential satisfaction.

Jacobs considered that "streets without eyes" or "the absence of the trust defined as casual public contact at a local level, a feeling of public identity of people, a resource in time of personal or neighborhood need, is a disaster to a city street."[38] Jacobs stressed the importance of social capital and suggested that good interpersonal relationships among neighbors would contribute to the vitality of the city neighborhoods and would increase residential satisfaction. Although results indicate that people (especially homeowners) who live in areas characterized by neighborliness have a higher level of neighborhood satisfaction, this analysis suggests that there are other factors that may have a stronger influence on one's positive perceptions of the urban environment than satisfaction with neighbors does.

Jacobs[39] also noted that "in orthodox city planning neighborhood open spaces are venerated in an amazingly uncritical fashion, much as savages venerate magical fetishes. (...) More Open Space for what? For muggings? For bleak vacuums between buildings?" The present analysis suggests that people might not "use city open space just because it is there and because city planners and designers wish they would," as Jacobs[40] argued. Results show that homeowners in particular, consider the amount of open space in a neighborhood an important characteristic of the place that has a significant influence on positive perceptions of local environment.

Different from Mumford, Jane Jacobs considered that high density areas would be beneficial for the cities and would make them more livable. An analysis of several empirical research studies showed, however, that contrary to the common assumption, density or crowding does not necessarily have either a negative or positive impact on urban life because the level of crowding is socially defined.[41] According to the theory of proxemics preferences for high or low densities are culturally based among people belonging to different ethnic groups. If, for instance, Italians seem to have a high-contact culture, Americans seem to prefer a good deal of space.[42] The Louisvillians' preference for open spaces might also suggest that one of the new principles of urban design in the United States, that "ruled that all space be controlled, all comings and goings be noted, and all corners be open to the light and to watchful eyes,"[43] was actually a reflection of public opinion. In addition, research showed that permanent open space increases nearby residential land values more than three times the value of an equivalent amount of developable open space.[44] Recent research also indicates that while childless couples tend to prefer living in relatively more dense, larger standard metropolitan statistical areas that provide easier access to services compared to suburban or rural areas, households with children prefer to live in low-density areas with easy access to green space and recreational opportunities,[45] suggesting that the Americans' preference for open spaces continues to be recorded.

Jacobs[46] contended that if conventional planning and land-use theory were true, "quiet and cleanliness" would have "as much positive effects as they are supposed to." The results of this analysis indicate that for both homeowners and renters, satisfaction with the amount of peace and quiet in the neighborhood and with the neighborhood's cleanliness level have positive effects on a person's level of neighborhood satisfaction. In addition, contrary to Jacobs's assumptions, Americans seem to be strongly influenced in their perceptions of the local urban environment by aesthetic considerations. A neighborhood's general appearance is a predictor that significantly influenced neighborhood satisfaction in both subsamples.

Jacobs focused in her work on the role neighborhoods might play in maintaining liveliness and vitality in a city. The author asserted that "even the most urbane citizen does care about the atmosphere of the street and district where he lives" and that "the common run of city people do depend greatly on their neighborhoods for the kind of everyday lives they lead."[47] Additional analyses not included here indicate that there are factors other than neighborhood satisfaction, which play an important role in structuring people's perceptions of the quality-of-life in a city, such as the quality of public services in the urban setting or housing satisfaction.

To summarize, despite its limitations, the present analysis did not find strong support for Jacobs's arguments regarding the conditions that should exist at the neighborhood level to make people feel content with their life in a city. Nonetheless, it might seem unfair to evaluate Jacobs's prescriptions and to discuss people's attitudes toward the urban environment expressed decades after the publication of *The Death and Life of Great American Cities* without taking into account all the major economic, social, and political changes that took place since the 1960s and kept affecting the American urban scene and also the way individuals were perceiving it. Discrepancies between reality and people's perceptions of their living space do certainly occur and people's satisfaction with their residential environment might be influenced by the alternatives they believe are available in a particular urban setting or by aspects of life that were not included in this analysis. Yet, it appears that those who recognized the prevalence of the American taste for "beauty, order, and spaciousness" were more properly anticipating the Americans' spatial environmental preferences than Jacobs did. And, Lewis Mumford was one of them.

Conclusion: The legacy of two great visionaries

Although their visions regarding an ideal urban space appeared to be different, Jane Jacobs and Lewis Mumford were both concerned with the future of the American city, and particularly with the human dimension of the urban space. Even if their ideas were not explicitly formulated in this direction, both authors were, in fact, interested in discovering the conditions that would improve the quality of life of urban residents. And both authors influenced at some degree the new urbanists' ideas about what livable urban communities should look like.

New urbanism supports a design-oriented approach to planned urban development and resembles the orientation of early planning theorists, such as Howard, Olmstead, and Geddes,[48] that Mumford admired. Jane Jacobs thought that we should think of cities as natural systems that need to be nurtured, that we should try to identify the essence of any city, and that we should try to understand what makes cities to work organically.[49] As Golberger recently noted, "the term *mixed use*, which started as a sharp-eyed writer's observation of what underlies an organic urban fabric, has become a developer's mantra."New Urbanist developments demonstrate that there is an effort to preserve or create mixed use neighborhoods in order to restore or generate vibrant neighborhoods, an aspect considered by Jacobs essential to optimal city life.[50]

Goldberger contended that the new urbanists' philosophy of returning to pedestrian-oriented cities seems to owe a lot to Jacobs.[51] However, Mumford also considered that adapting planning decisions to the needs of the car is dangerous for the social health of the city. Jacobs's arguments in support of higher population density and diversity, mixed housing, or preservation of traditional neighborhood structures were adopted by the new urbanism's proponents as well. Jacobs and Mumford both argued that old traditional neighborhoods should be rehabilitated and revitalized. Because of their ideas, many distressed urban neighborhoods are more likely to be gentrified than cleared for redevelopment.[52]

Jacobs opposed the separation of uses that characterized traditional zoning regulations and introduced the concept "zoning for diversity," anticipating what new urbanists refer to as sustainable forms of development based on mixed-use zoning.[53] Yet, Dreier argued that although advocates of *smart growth* and *new urbanism* claim nowadays Jacobs's mantle, she might dispute some of their approaches, particularly their failure to "make room for poor and working-class folks."[54] According to Goldberger, Jacobs found the new urbanists "hopelessly suburban"[55] and she might agree with Fainstein[56], who in her critique of the new urbanism noted that "the movement is less convincing in its approach to social injustice" by proposing "a different form of suburbia" that did not succeed to overcome metropolitan social segregation."In addition, Fainstein argued that if one visits "planned new town and downtown redevelopment projects, even those built with commitments to diversity and community, one is struck by their physical and social homogeneity."[57] Interviewed in 2000, by James Kunstler, a writer, social critic, and leading supporter of the new urbanism movement, Jane

Jacobs expressed her views on new urbanism and even made some predictions:

> I do not think that we are to be saved by new developments done to
> New Urbanist principles. (…) I am very glad that New Urbanists are
> educating America. I think that when this takes hold and when
> enough of the old regulations can be gotten out of the way, which is
> what is holding things up, there is going to be some great period of
> infilling. And a lot of that will be make-shift and messy and it won't
> measure up to New Urbanist ideas of design. But it will measure up
> to a lot of their other philosophy. And in fact if there isn't a lot of this
> popular and make-shift infilling, the suburbs will never get
> corrected.[58]

In her later writings, "Jacobs touted the role of the cities as the engines of economic prosperity. In doing so, she anticipated arguments against unfettered suburban sprawl, recent debates about the reliance of suburbs on healthy cities, and the new wave of thinking about regionalism."[59] Without doubt, Lewis Mumford and Jane Jacobs both contributed significantly to the definition of the American urbanism and to the way we perceive our cities. Although it is difficult to imagine how these two thinkers, who belong to different cultural streams would react today to the new direction in planning theory that the new urbanism movement proposed or to the way their ideas have been put in practice by the new urbanists, it is probably not unrealistic to assume that Mumford and Jacobs would both approve the neotraditionalists' appreciation for traditional architecture and urban forms. Both writers might also praise the new urbanists' efforts to offer better alternatives to "suburban monotony and bland modernism"[60] and their hopeful quest for an improved quality of urban life.

Notes

1. P. L. Lawrence, The Unknown Jane Jacobs: Geographer, Propagandist, City Planning Idealist (pp. 15-36). In Page, M. & Mennel, T. (eds.) Reconsidering Jane Jacobs, (Washington, D. C.: APA Planners Press, 2011).
2. P. Goldberger, Uncommon Sense: Remembering Jane Jacobs, who Wrote the 20th Century Most Influential Book about Cities. The American Scholar, Autumn 2006.Avaialble at http://theamericanscholar.org/uncomon-sense/
3. See E. Talen, *New Urbanism and American Planning: The Conflict of Cultures* (New York: Routledge, 2005, p.1).
4. J. Jacobs, *The Death and Life of Great American Cities* (New York: Vintage Books, 1961).
5. P. Goldberger, *op.cit.*
6. C. Klemek, Dead or Alive at Fifty? Reading Jane Jacobs on her Golden Anniversary, *Dissent*, 58(2), 2011, pp. 75-79.
7. J. J. Palen, *The Urban World*. Third Edition (New York: McGrow - Hill Book Company, 1987, p. 321).
8. P. Goldberger, *op.cit.*
9. See L. Mumford, *The City in History,* (New York: Harvest Books, 1961).
10. Goldberger, *op. cit.*

11. Z. A. Miller & P. M. Melvin, *TheUrbanization of Modern America. A Brief History.* Second Edition (New York: Harcourt Brace Jovanovich, Publishers, 1987, p. 201).

12. H. M. Choldin,. Retrospective Review Essay: Neighborhood Life and Urban Environment, *American Journal of Sociology* 84(2), 1978, pp. 457-463.

13. Goldberger, *op. cit.*

14. See P. Dreier, Jane Jacobs' Radical Legacy, *Shelterforce Online*, Issue 146, Summer 2006. Available at: http://www.nhi.org/online/issues/146/janejacobslegacy.html.

15. In the 1960s in response to such programs as urban renewal and highway construction which displaced hundreds of thousands of poor and minority urban residents, Paul Davidoff introduced the notion of "advocacy planning." and the group (Suburban Action) he initiated, became a leader in combating exclusionary suburban zoning. Advocacy planning played an important role in reforming urban renewal and urban highway planning by requiring greater citizen participation, improved relocation guarantees, and neighborhood preservation. See R. Steinbacher, R. & V. O. Benson (eds) *Introduction to Urban Studies* (Dubuque, Iowa: Kendall/Hunt Publishing Company, 1995, pp.163-164).

16. C. N. Glaab & A. T. Brown, *A History of Urban America.* Third Edition. (New York: Macmillan & Co., 1983, p. 309).

17. Jacobs, *op. cit.*

18. Palen, *op.cit.*

19. Jacobs, *op. cit.,* p. 32.

20. Jacobs, *op. cit.,* p. 31.

21. See Choldin, *op.cit.*

22. M. Bookchin, *The Limits of the City.* Second Edition. (Montreal: Black Rose Books, 1991, p. 406).

23. Palen, *op.cit.*, p.321.

24. Choldin, *op.cit.,* p. 457.

25. L. Mumford, Home Remedies for Urban Cancer, in L. K. Loewenstein (ed.) *Urban Studies. An Introductory Reader.* (New York: The Free Press, 1971, pp.385-404).

26. Glaab & Brown, *op. cit.*, p. 288.

27. Glaab & Brown, *op. cit.*, p. 296.

28. E. Talen, *New Urbanism and American Planning: The Conflict of Cultures,* (New York: Routledge, 2005, p. 10).

29. See Jane Jacobs Interviewed by Jim Kunstler for Metropolis Magazine, March 2001; http://www.kunstler.com/mags_jacobs.htm.

30. Mumford, *op.cit.*, p. 389.

31. Mumford, *op. cit.*,p.390.

32. Mumford, *op. cit.*,p.390.

33. Mumford, *op. cit.*, p. 392.

34. Jacobs, *op.cit.*, p.372.

35. Mumford, *op. cit.*, p. 396.

36. Talen, *op.cit.*, p.10.

37. See Ben-Chien Liu, *Quality of Life Indicators in U.S. Metropolitan Areas: A Statistical Analysis* (New York: Praeger, 1976). Using data collected in five defined areas (economic, political environmental, health and education, and social), based on indicators assumed to reflect quality of life, Liu compared sixty-five American cities of 500,000 or more in population, eighty-three cities of between 200,000 and 500,000, and ninety-five cities of between 50,000 and 200,000 people. After a total score computed by summing up individual scores for each of the five components, Liu ranked all the cities included in his analysis assigning them the following grades: outstanding, excellent, good, adequate, and substandard. According to this classification, Louisville, one of the sixty-five largest cities

of the United States, ranked fifty-three. Newark, Detroit, Atlanta, St. Louis, Pittsburgh, and Baltimore were some of the other seventeen cities included in the same "adequate" category.

38. Jacobs, *op.cit.*, p.56.

39. Jacobs, *op. cit.* p.90.

40. Jacobs, *op. cit.* p.90.

41. Palen, *op.cit.*, p.169.

42. Choldin, *op. cit.*, p.462.

43. M. Gladwell, Open Spaces... Fear of Crime is Removing Intimacy from Today's Cities, *The Courier Journal*, April 2, 1995.

44. J. Geoghegan, The value of open spaces in residential land use. *Land Use Policy* 19, no. 1: 91-98, 2002.

45. See K. Tae-Kyung, M. W. Horner, and R. W. Marans, Life cycle and environmental factors in selecting residential and job locations. *Housing Studies* 20, no. 3: 457-73, 2005; I. Fjortoft& J. Sageie, The natural environment as a playground for children: Landscape description and analyses of a natural playscape. *Landscape and Urban Planning* 48: 83-97, 2000.

46. Jacobs, *op. cit.* p.258.

47. Jacobs, *op. cit.* p.117.

48. See S. Fainstein, New Directions in Planning Theory, *Urban Affairs Review*, 35(4): 451-478, 2000.

49. Goldberger, *op. cit.*

50. J. Grant, *Planning the Good Community: New Urbanism in Theory and Practice.* (London: Routledge, 2006).

51. Goldberger, *op.cit.*

52. See Klemek, op. cit.; M. Lind, Urban Philosopher: A Walking Tour of Lewis Mumford, December 30, 1999, *New America Foundation*, http://newamerica.net/node/5660.

53. M. Wendt, The Importance of Death and Life of the American Great Cities (1961) by Jane Jacobs to the Profession of Urban Planning. *New Visions for Public Affairs*, Vol. 1, Spring 2009, pp. 1-24.

54. Dreier, *op. cit.*

55. See Goldberger, *op.cit.*

56.Fainstein, *op.cit.*, p.463-464.

57.Fainstein, *op.cit.*, p.464.

58. Jane Jacobs Interviewed by Jim Kunstler for Metropolis Magazine, 2001.

59. Dreier, *op. cit.*

60. See Fainstein, *op.cit.*, p. 466.

Chapter Three

We're on a Road to Nowhere: Housing Policy in the U.S.

Karl Besel

We shall solve the City Problem by leaving the City. —Henry Ford (1922)

When my Midwestern born and raised friends and relatives ask me what it was like to grow up in Southern California, I often reply that it was great, besides the fact that I spent most of my childhood in a car. If the Talking Heads had released their hit single by the late 1970s, I'm sure I would have spent my prime soccer and baseball years humming "We're on a Road to Nowhere" in the backseat of some parents' car as I was schlepped away to a game. While the drive was often no more than a few miles from my school, it could take up to a half hour, depending upon the traffic. If I was being chauffeured by another parent, she/he typically took the freeway whenever possible. Since by mom, a Montana farm girl, was terrified by these massive urban spider webs, she insisted on taking the neighborhood streets. Inevitably, we were typically late showing up to games when my mom drove since her approach took significantly longer-in my teenage mind, an eternity! Either way, all these commutes were remarkably uneventful; all the freeways, streets, neighborhoods, and homes seemed the same to me. After my family moved to a suburb of Cleveland when I was fifteen (yes, I hated my parents for a while after that), I discovered that the Midwest had a lot in common with Southern California. Sure, the kids dressed funny, were more likely to smoke, and said "Bogus!" way too much. These differences aside, the neighborhood design and architecture was pretty much the same as what I remembered of suburban Los Angeles. The relatively larger home and lot size didn't take away from the fact that all the homes within both regions of the country were boxy with bland exterior molding, and exhibited multi-angled roofs. The neighborhood designs possessed even more similarities. The streets were generally wide with homes set back away from the streets. Cul-de-sacs were at the end of the block, and sidewalk construction was sporadic. The lack of walking and biking paths made these types of transportation frustrating, and often treacherous. Subsequently, owning a car (or having parents that owned a car) was a necessary part of daily existence in both suburban Los Angeles, and suburban Cleveland. The weather was much better in the South Bay area, but both areas shared the same dependence on the automobile for all elements of an adolescent's life-clothes, entertainment, school, and food.

All these similarities between the sun baked suburb of Torrance, California, I left and the cloudy, rainy, sleety, and snowy suburb of North Olmsted, Ohio, I moved to under duress were taken for granite. Nothing else I encountered in life at that point made me think a different type of community existed. My first experience with life outside of this "Suburban Nation" existence was during a semester spent overseas at the Valparaiso University Study Center in Cambridge. The Center itself straddled a former Roman built road, which weaved its way along some of the older and larger "colleges" that were homes to many Cambridge University, UK, students. As with most American students that spend a semester in Europe, I was initially impressed with the architecture and subsequent efforts put into preserving grand old buildings. After establishing a daily routine of attending classes, getting groceries, and amusing myself in general, I was equally impressed with the ease in which these regular activities were carried out. Virtually all of my needs (and many wants) were accessible via a fifteen-twenty minute walk. As a starving college student, I also found that while the cost of living may have been somewhat higher in terms of the price of food, I could find great deals at the farmer's market which took place every Saturday morning. In addition, the fact that I didn't need to own a car made the general cost of living less than what I encountered later attending college within the greater Chicago area. As I began to meet other college students that lived in British cities such as London, Birmingham, and Manchester, I quickly found out that the lack of (or often complete absence) automobile dependence experienced by students went beyond the university town scene. Frequently I met individuals over the age of 25 that didn't possess a driver's license, and subsequently had no desire to apply for this "privilege." Certainly I never encountered any young people like this in America. The beautiful architecture, accessible eating and entertainment venues, relative ease of life at an affordable cost made me think that the American dream, which essentially is the Suburban dream, was void of much of the quality of life I was experiencing in England. The following quote from James Howard Kunstler's book captures many of the sentiments I shared with my fellow American students:

> Anybody who travels back and forth across the Atlantic has to be impressed with the differences between European cities and ours, which make it appear as if World War II actually took place in Detroit and Washington rather than Berlin and Rotterdam.[1]

How could it be that we may have grown up in communities that were so different from European ones? Ironically enough, our grandparents' generation was a key part of rebuilding many of the European cities destroyed during World War II, under the post-war Marshall Plan. How could it be that we subsidized a massive construction effort so that other people could experience a higher quality of life than we do? Americans may be generous and benevolent, but that's downright crazy! The answer to this question is of course, complicated. Nonetheless, I will highlight some federal policies of the 20th Century, as well as some differences between how Americans and Europeans value urban planning efforts, in order to guide an examination of these questions.

The Suburban Nation Dream Begins: New Deal Style

Does anyone suppose that, in real life, answers to any of the great questions that worry us today are going to come out of homogeneous settlements?

—Jane Jacobs, *The Death and Life of Great American Cities (1961)*

If your grandparents or great-grandparents set out to buy a home in 1930, they would have saved up to 50 percent of the purchase price for a down payment and applied at their local bank for a five-year mortgage. People bought houses in this manner in 1930 because that's how banks did business. During the New Deal, Franklin Roosevelt's Federal Housing Administration (FHA) pioneered a new form of mortgage, which required only 20 percent down and let the borrower repay over 30 years. At the time what the FHA created was looked upon as being very innovative (and American) since the marketplace was structured in a way that fulfilled a public purpose. Following World War II a combination of the 30 year mortgage, GI Bill, as well as an unprecedented increase in per capita income led millions of Americans to vacate cities for the suburbs.[2] The mixed feelings some young professionals feel today about living a historical home in the inner city to raise a family within the better school districts of a nearby suburb was unthinkable to our grandparents. In their pre Environmental Protection Agency, pre historical preservation era, cities offered nothing but higher crime, factory pollution, poor schools, and a limited number of recreational amenities. Governmental policies that encouraged lending to middle class professionals during the 1930s and 1940s were extended to most Americans beginning the 1970s with the Community Reinvestment Act (CRA). This piece of federal legislation encouraged commercial bank and savings associations to offer more mortgages within low and moderate income neighborhoods. CRA was expanded several times during the 1990s, as the federal government pressured Fannie Mae, the nation's biggest underwriter of home mortgages, to aggressively promote lending to lower income individuals. The federal government's zealous encouragement of home ownership coincided with a deregulation trend which started with the Reagan administration. This trend towards limited governmental oversight of the mortgage system couldn't have come at a worse time, since the banking industry was experiencing a substantial transformation. Twenty years ago, a bank originated a loan, serviced the loan, and then collected the repayment. The 1990s gave birth to securitization, where many loans were originated, packaged into pools and then sliced and diced into bonds to be sold off to third party investors. In the aftermath of the housing and credit bubble, we now see that many of the systems used in this process were inadequate and fraught with special interests, self-dealing and conflicts of interest.[3]

Eisenhower and Industrial Era Planners: Partners in Sprawl

If federal housing policy related to mortgage lending practices led to sprawling suburbs, Eisenhower Era policies and modernist architecture shaped the sprawl. The Federal Aid Highway Act (FAHA) of 1956, along with the Civil Defense Committee, provided a legal framework for the creation of a 42,000 mile interstate highway system. The prescription of this system was straightforward: street design must facilitate evacuation before and cleanup after, a major "nuclear event." The desire for increased traffic volume-"unimpeded flow," has resulted in wider streets. While travel lanes on old streets are often only nine feet wide or less, new streets are usually required to have twelve-foot lanes, which take longer for pedestrians to cross. Unimpeded flow also has another name-speeding; adding more to pedestrian risk.[4]

In addition to ensuring that cars would always be granted priority over pedestrians, Cold War transportation policies encouraged highway construction at any price. Since FAHA provided 90 percent of the cost of interstates, state and city officials never had to worry about the "real" cost of this heavily federally subsided program. Robert Moses may have been the first prominent public official to destroy older neighborhoods in the name of interstate and interstate "progress," but he certainly wasn't the last. Virtually every American city fell prey to the interstate monster that destroyed neighborhoods and displaced hundreds of thousands of citizens to make way for a new system that placed the needs of automobiles over the needs of humans. As described by Duany et al (2000), of those streets that somehow escaped the widening influences of the traffic-flow and Cold War lobbies, many are currently falling prey to the access requirements of the fire departments. Their new standards, which shorten emergency vehicle response time at the expense of all other criteria, are typically designed to accommodate the most ambitious of maneuvers. While these policies may make short term sense, they fail to consider some longer term safety needs. Firstly, they put more weight on fire rescue than on prevention of injury in general; they try to minimize emergency response time, without considering that the resulting wide streets lead to an increased number of traffic accidents, since people drive faster on them. Fire departments have yet to acknowledge that fire safety is but a small part of a much larger picture that others refer to as life safety. The biggest threat to life safety is not fires but car accidents, by a tremendous margin. The second mistake fire departments make is purchasing oversized trucks that experience problems in maneuvering through anything but the widest streets. Sometimes these trucks are required by outdated union regulations, but often they are simply the result of a town's desire to have the most effective machinery it can afford. Unfortunately once these pricey vehicles are purchased, the truck turns from servant to master, making all but the most wasteful and unpleasant street spaces impossible.[5]

The Rise and Fall of the McMansion and Cookie Cutter Neighborhoods

Unscrupulous developers and realtors have been quick to take advantage of the federally subsidized interstate and highway systems that strangle the American countryside and cityscapes like a massive spider web. As foreclosure rates for millions of these properties continue to climb, many are left to wonder, what was the attraction to this blasé architecture and neighborhood design in the first place? Like its culinary counterpart, the McMansion provides excellent value for its price. American homebuilders are probably the best in the world when it comes to providing individuals with a maximum number of bathrooms and bedrooms per square foot. In tandem with its food equivalent, these affordable yet hastily built homes may be initially easy on the pocketbook, but the long term costs of longer commutes, higher traffic levels, and isolation from amenities leads to greater financial, as well as psychological costs. A Big Mac may be cheap, but no health care professional would recommend perpetuating this fast food indulgence into a lifestyle. For this reason the developers of sprawl have been reviled characters, making pimps, prostitutes, and even attorneys look good by comparison. This may seem short sided since developers provide the nation with a wide variety of products, often at great financial risk. They build houses, shops, offices, streets, and roads. Nonetheless, they are unable to provide these things in the form of towns; they can only offer sprawl. It was not always this way. In fact, until 1945 American planners and developers were often revered by the citizens within the communities they built, and at times by the nation as a whole. For example, Alexandria, Virginia, is often praised by urban planning scholars for its use of narrow, versatile streets, mixed use buildings, and pedestrian friendly downtown area. This classic "American" city was laid by George Washington when he was seventeen years of age. When George Merrick built Florida's Coral Gables only eighty years ago, he was regarded not as a developer but as a town founder. A bust in his likeness still presides proudly over City Hall. Other "famed" developers include J.C. Nicols in Kansas City, James Oglethorpe in Savannah, Mary Emery in Mariemont, Ohio, as well as a myriad of other developers nationwide that built their communities before World War II. The historical lesson here is build a town and you will probably be admired by current and future generations. Build sprawl and your legacy will not be a pleasant one.[6]

Signs of Policy Paradigm Shifts

Sprawl, in the form of low density housing development, continues to be the preferred method for housing and community building within most parts of the United States. In general, new proposals for lower density development are more likely to be approved by planning commissions than their higher density counterparts in states such as Indiana. Subsequently, mixed use buildings which are a key component of new urbanism communities such as Seaside, Florida, and the Village of West Clay, Indiana, would be illegal within the vast majority of suburban tracks in their respective states. Despite the fact that federal, state and local policies still favor sprawl building over town building directly through subsidizing road and highway construction, as well as zoning regulations, and indirectly by approving lower density development projects more often than higher density ones, there are some signs that the policy pendulum is beginning to swing in another direction.

The principles of new urbanism got a significant boost when Henry Cisneros, former secretary of the U.S. Department of Housing and Urban Development (HUD), signed the Charter of the New Urbanism in May, 1996. Cisneros has also initiated a "Homeownership Zones" program offering grants and loans to cities for redevelopment based on new urbanist principles. These strategies were also adopted in Hope IV, a program initiated by HUD in order to apply these traditional town development strategies within areas occupied by high rise housing projects.[7] One of the first and most innovative of these projects was Louisville's Villages of Park DuValle community. This project consisted of a partnership between the City of Louisville, nonprofit developer Community Builders, and HUD via the HOPE IV program. This 1994 project achieved such a high degree of success in revitalizing a formerly blighted and crime ridden inner city area that it paved the way for a similar project initiated just a few years called Liberty Green.[8] In tandem with Park DuValle, Liberty Green was built on the former site of a housing project, and now features a mix of condos, apartments, and Greek Revival style single family homes which line narrow streets in the front and alleys in the back. A key commonality between these communities built within existing urban areas, and their counterparts in new suburban developments, is the marketplace that has surfaced for new urbanist design. The numbers speak for themselves on the market demand for these communities. In 1996 there were only 119 new urbanism projects in the U.S.; by 2004 the number skyrocketed to 648 nationwide. Subsequently, new urbanism seems to be catching on in other countries as well. Architects and planners in Britain, Canada, France, India, Indonesia, Japan, and Turkey are adopting the principles of new urbanism to design the built environment.[9] In light of the success of some of the first inner city projects such as Park DuValle, coupled with substantial market demand, it appears likely that national housing policies will continue to be influenced by new urbanism principles.

Within the American federalist system of government, the policies and mandates of Washington D.C. are not enough to catalyze lasting change. City and suburban mayors, as well as planning commissions and economic development organizations, often serve as the primary implementers of these policies. As mayor of Louisville in the 1990s, Jerry Abramson worked diligently and tenaciously to form partnerships and subsequent revenue streams to jump start the Village of Park DuValle project. Urban based projects such as Park DuValle typically rely on federal funding to initiate development, since raising private capital for inner city revitalization projects is very challenging, if not impossible. After the City of Louisville's initial proposal to secure federal empowerment zone funds was rejected, Abramson and his city were successful in securing seed funds from HUD enterprise zone funds to begin the Park DuValle project.[10] Especially during these times of soaring federal deficits and subsequent cutbacks for most taxpayer supported programs, mayors and city officials need to be both persistent and thick skinned in leveraging funding for new urbanist projects. On the other end of the spectrum, suburban mayors such as Jim Brainard rallied support for the Brenwick development team when they proposed to build the first new urbanism community of its kind in Indiana.[11] Brenwick's developer Tom Huston and former director of operations Jose Kruetz saw Mayor Brainard's support of their new and controversial project as "a key part" of their ability to gain approval from an initially apprehensive planning commission.[12] While Brenwick's Village of West Clay was a one of a kind community when it was initiated in 1999, developers George Sweet and Tom Huston actually represented the "second generation" of investors in new urbanism who were hoping to capitalize on the financial successes of the first generation of neotraditional developers. These pioneers included Robert Davis (Seaside), Joe Alfandre (Kentlands), Phil Angelides (Laguna West), Vince Graham (Newpoint), Henry Turley (Harbortown), and Michael Eisner (Celebration). These individuals were all motivated primarily by a desire to provide a better place to live and only secondarily by profit. If this generation finds traditional neighborhood development to be a better investment than sprawl, as it has so far, it is reasonable to expect that the development industry as a whole will follow suit.[13]

In sum, there is a growing expectation in the development community that new zoning ordinances and land-use regulations at all levels of government will be more supportive of new urbanism. However, it will take time before such policies are extensively enacted at the federal and state levels, and implemented by local officials. Fortunately as more and more business leaders, public officials, and average citizens begin to view town building as the best antidote for ending sprawl, the tide seems to be changing course.

Notes

1. J.H. Kunstler, *Home from Nowhere: Remaking Our Everyday World for the Twenty-first Century,* (New York: Simon and Schuster, 1996).

2. D. Osborne and T. Gaebler, *Reinventing Government: How the Entrepreneurial Spirit is Transforming the Public Sector,* (New York: Penguin Books, 1992).

3. Alex Zikakis, "A Long Time in the Making," Capstone Advisors, December 2008 Report.

4. A. Duany, E. Plater-Zyberk, and J. Speck, *Suburban Nation: The Rise of Sprawl and the Decline of the American Dream,* (New York: North Point Press, 2000).

5. Duany et al, *op. cit.*

6. Duany et al, *op. cit.*

7. Ajay Garde, "Designing and Developing New Urbanist Projects in the United States: Insights and Implications," *Journal of Urban Design,* Vol. 11, No. 1, (2006): 33-54.

8. Mayor Jerry Abramson, interview by Karl Besel, 2009.

9. New Urbanism News (n.d.) Available at http://www.newurbanismnews.com/, accessed December 15th, 2004.

10. Abramson, *op. cit.*

11. Mayor Jim Brainard, interview by Karl Besel, 2009.

12. Tom Huston and Jose Kruetz, interviews by Karl Besel, 2009.

13. Duany et al, *op. cit.*

Chapter Four

A Case for Traditional Town Planning

Karl Besel and John Vick

Why Mumford and Duany Like the Georgetowns of the World

Lewis Mumford in many ways is like the coach many of us had growing up who dispensed praise in a very limited and efficient manner. When one receives a complement from this type of hardnosed coach, you know he means it. Like the coach we may have loved to hate but probably held in high esteem, Mumford is relentless in *The City in History*, (1961) when it comes to tearing apart the design (or his perceived lack thereof) of many American cities. Even Washington D.C., which is considered one of the best planned American cities, is not spared from criticism by Mumford. Here's what the award winning urban scholar had to say about the nation's capital:

> The assumed right of the private motor car to go any place in the city and park anywhere is nothing less than a license to destroy the city. L'Enfant's plan, by its very invitation to traffic, has now proved its own worst enemy. (*The City in History*, p. 408)

Mumford was critical of the Beltway's baroque planning scheme, something he perceived as encouraging automobile dependence, as well as inducing unmanageable traffic problems. Anyone who has driven on the Beltway during rush-hour would have to agree that Mumford has a point. While critical of L'Enfant's design, he praised Georgetown for its "narrow streets and its more compact layout, modest enough to service in the 19th century for the little dwellings of mechanics and tradesmen. The area has been converted, during the last generation, into an upper-class residential neighborhood. There one gratefully finds, not the monumental, but the domestic scale."[1]

Andres Duany, the famous Cuban-born architect and most prominent exponent of neotraditional design, is more generous with L'Enfant's planning strategies in his co-authored book *Suburban Nation*, (2000). The planning philosophies of Mumford and Duany converge in their writings about how Georgetown has been able to embody the principles of sustainable town planning. The plan is sustainable since it has effectively adapted to both economic and social changes over the last two centuries, as noted by Mumford. Subsequently, there continues to be market demand for both commercial and residential uses within this neighborhood. The principles of sustainable town planning shared by Mumford and Duany are detailed as follows:

Diversity of Incomes: For over a century, neighborhood blocks within Georgetown have housed people of widely divergent incomes. As noted by Duany et al (2000), there are rental apartment buildings that house schoolteachers, clerks, and recent college graduates. Within townhomes a variety of young professionals reside, as well as some retirees who may rent out basement apartments to secretaries, day care workers, and students. Subsequently, Georgetown features a number of mansions that are owned by some of the great fortunes of the Mid-Atlantic. These elegant properties often include carriage houses and garage apartments the grounds that my house artists, architects, and other members of the intentionally poor. An astute observer will notice that there is a certain form of segregation within these neighborhood blocks: apartments face apartments, townhomes face townhomes, and mansions face mansions. Housing types are segregated by street, with the transition always occurring at mid-block, where backyards meet. Like the suburban system, this technique preserves property values and ensures a consistent streetscape. Unlike the suburban system, it does not isolate people from one another.

Essentially Georgetown is a microcosm of American society. As discussed within Chapter 1, Mumford admired how Greek villages and cities intermingled housing for the rich and poor in a similar fashion; a characteristic which embraces the spirit of democracy within both ancient and modern societies. Unfortunately most suburban development in the U.S. is geared towards segregating people based upon their income and wealth. The most extreme examples of this type of segregation by incomes are manifested within gated communities. By the late 1990s, the number of these gated communities had risen to 20,000, holding more than 3 million housing units. Their popularity seems to be greatest in Southern California, where 54 percent of home shoppers wanted a home in a "gated, walled development."[2] These fiefdoms for the wealthy could be considered elitism on steroids, where the richer members of a community insist on isolating themselves from all members of society by cloistering in McMansions behind medieval like walls. In contrast to their Dark Age counterparts, castle walls within European society were intended to protect all members of a particular community, not just the rich.

Mixed Use: Anyone that has visited Georgetown is familiar with the wide range of restaurant choices available along the main drag which cuts through this historical neighborhood. These restaurants and other retail and service oriented businesses are just a few minutes away from many residents of the area. This mix of both residential and commercial uses is not only unheard of within most suburban areas — it's also considered illegal.[3] Most suburban developments only allow for one type of construction: single family homes. A variety of rationales can be provided for this occurrence, with the primary one being that mixed use negatively impacts property values. As demonstrated by the Georgetown neighborhood, City of Alexandria, and a host of other historical urban neighborhoods throughout the East Coast and Midwest, mixed use planning, especially within historically significant areas, probably enhances property values. Duany et al (2000) also found that new urbanism communities in suburban areas exhibit rates of real estate appreciation which are higher than their suburban counterparts. Subsequently, mixing residential and commercial uses within a particular neighborhood makes for a better quality of life for its citizens. Older residents and younger families alike are provided with greater access to grocery stores and restaurants with this model. Thus, what is considered illegal within most American suburbs enhances property values and in general, quality of life, within many historic and new urbanism communities.

Narrower Streets: Parking your car in Georgetown is not always easy, especially for those not accustomed to parallel parking. If you think parking is challenging, try driving along Georgetown's narrow streets in a large vehicle. This 200 year old neighborhood was built with pedestrians in mind in light of the era when its plan was crafted. Narrower streets not only encourage residents to walk more, they end up being significantly safer than wider streets. Subsequently, the large curb radius which goes along with wider streets doubles both pedestrian crossing distance and automobile speed.[4]

Inclusion of walkways: The residential neighborhoods within Georgetown feature homes and apartments that sit close to the sidewalk and plainly face forward. Jane Jacobs was one of the first supporters of the safety implications of this type of traditional housing scheme. Her concept of having more "eyes on the street" as a vehicle for crime reduction was subsequently discussed in greater detail by Oscar Newman in *Defensible Space*. Within this classic urban theory text, Newman argues that in order to discourage crime, a street space must be watched over by buildings with doors and windows facing it. Walls, fences, and locks are all less effective at deterring crime than a simple lit window.[5] Interestingly, no one needs to be standing in the window, as the window takes on a human presence of its own. Since *Defensible Space* was written in 1969, the efficacy of many of the book's concepts has been demonstrated through a number of rigorous studies. Many of these concepts are now promulgated under an imprimatur coined Crime Prevention Through Environmental Design (CPTED).[6]

Green space Planning: This historic neighborhood not only impresses first time visitors with stately and charming architecture, but also with an ample supply of tree lined walkways and parks. Washington D.C. is known for its many parks and monuments; one of the oldest green spaces includes the old canal area turned tourist attraction within Georgetown. In tandem with planning for pedestrian use through the systematic use of sidewalks, sustainable neighborhood plans also need to make green spaces a priority. The considerable growth in the number of landscape architecture course offerings within American universities speaks to the consumer demand for professionally developed and maintained park systems. Frederick Olmsted is probably the most famous of the American landscape architects and the homes built along his parks in cities such as New York (Central Park) and Louisville (Cherokee Park) continue to be some of the most expensive properties in their respective cities. City dwellers have always considered close proximity to a park a significant amenity, and as demonstrated by these cities, the more affluent members of society are willing to pay a premium to reside along these planned green spaces.

Efficiencies Resulting from High Density Living

Neighborhoods such as Georgetown are more than just pretty and safer places to work and live-these neighborhoods end up being more cost effective than their low density counterparts. As cities and towns throughout the U.S. are laying off teachers in mass, and entire states such as California are on the verge of bankruptcy, elected officials don't have the luxury of spending taxpayer money on mere aesthetics-they need to demonstrate cost savings. Nonetheless, when you ask Mayor Brainard of Carmel why his city selected a high density model for redeveloping the downtown and surrounding neighborhoods, he discusses costs first, and quality of life second. "You just can't justify the costs spent on highways. We just got done spending 7-8 million per mile on the redevelopment of a county road with a bridge. The average cost of highway construction is 5 million per mile. Since most of these new roads are built along two to three acre lots, you don't have a lot of people paying for the roads," stated the Carmel mayor in a recent interview.[7] Brainard and many other mayors of suburban municipalities across America have found that the high level of public to private expenditure costs makes it difficult to justify the price tag of many new growth plans. Mayor Brainard's realization that high density development was more cost effective for his city has long been supported by comprehensive studies on the American automobile subsidy conducted by researchers such as Hart and Spivak (1993). Their analysis found that government subsidies for highways and parking alone amount to between 8 and 10 percent of our gross national product, the equivalent of a fuel tax of approximately $3.50 per gallon. If this tax were to account for "soft costs" such as pollution cleanup and emergency medical treatment, it would be as high as $9.00 per gallon. The cost of these subsidies, approximately $5,000 per car per year, is passed directly to the American citizen in the form of increased prices for products or, more often, as income, property, and sales taxes.[8]

In addition to the high tax burden placed on taxpayers for low density development, some developers are coming to the realization that changing demographics, and fall out over the subprime loan crisis, means sprawl ends up being a poor business decision, even in the short term. As baby boomers age in tandem with increases in the number of younger families and single adults, smart developers must find ways to serve many different market segments at once. In a typical suburb an independent pod must be built for each market segment since different incomes must never mix. In contrast to low density development, higher density development is more efficient for the developer since every market segment can be served through the construction of a single mixed-use area, thus limiting the infrastructure. Subsequently, high density neighborhoods include "starter," "move-up," "family," and "retirement" style homes.[9]

Factory Town Planning

In terms of building neighborhoods which provide a high quality of life which being cost effective to both the resident and taxpayer, high density development may seem to be a "no-brainer." Historically, high density development within cities typically came in the form of overcrowded apartments and poorly constructed homes ruled over by slumlords. Thus, for most of the history of city building, high density development had more to do with exploiting the poor than providing higher living standards. For example, shady landlords during the Roman Era found ways of subdividing old quarters into even narrower cells in order to maximize their profits. Mumford purported that "Neolithic villagers" were better off than these Roman artisans and laborers who lived in smaller and less sanitary dwellings than their prehistoric ancestors.[10] Conditions for many new immigrants to big American cities such as New York, Boston, or Chicago at the turn of the 20th weren't much better. Urban planners responded to the filthy, disease producing conditions which often resulted from having factories located too close to neighborhoods, by zoning urban areas for specific functions. Separating incompatible uses such as manufacturing and residential was very appropriate if not necessary at the turn of the century, but this urban planning scheme is outdated. At the dawn of the 21st Century, even quintessential blue collar cities such as Pittsburg and Cleveland have replaced their steel mills with much cleaner and quieter businesses. Duany aptly observed that the main purpose of single use planning in our post-industrial age seems to be to "make cars happy" by building more roads, highways, and parking lots to serve automotive needs at the expense of pedestrians.[11] An example this evolution in manufacturing can be found within the new urbanism community of Poundbury. This development includes factories that are built adjacent to residential districts. Poundbury's mixed use "experiment," which probably would have been considered inhumane 100 years ago, represents a trend towards fostering higher living standards by locating places of work closer to residential communities.[12]

Learning to Love Alleys

In tandem with the negative perceptions many Americans associate with living in a higher density area, alleys have also received a bad reputation. Expressions such as "you wouldn't want to meet him at the end of a dark alley" conjure up imagines of these narrow lanes being dangerous and undesirable places. In light of this negative connotation, it's no surprise that typical suburbs do not include alleys on the back of a developed block. Even designers of new urbanism neighborhoods encounter resistance when prospective residents are asked if they would consider living in a neighborhood with alleys. For example, the developers of the Village of West Clay found through focus groups with potential residents that most of the participants "did not desire to live in a neighborhood with alleys." In order to address this negative perception, developer Tom Huston reported "we decided to use the term lanes instead of alleys" to better market these side and back street areas to potential buyers.[13] Duany in *Suburban Nation* tells a similar story of the first time his planning team designed a neighborhood with alleys; they had to label them "jogging paths" in order to secure approval from the planning commission.[14] Despite these perceptions, alleys are actually one of the best innovations of traditional neighborhood planning. Alleys improve upon neighborhood safety, green space development, and aesthetics in the following ways:

Safety and Access: Instead of being places where crimes occur, alleys are actually more likely to be a factor in the saving of lives. Alleys are appreciated by fire chiefs since they allow firefighters with another path to buildings and homes. In addition to greater access related to safety, alleys can provide access to backyard rental spaces/granny flats, giving them an address independent of the main house. This greater access to homes and businesses coincides with better management of traffic flow. Alleys provide alternative routes to homes and businesses, and may be the quickest way to arrive at a particular destination for those familiar with the neighborhood.[15]

Green space Development: In order to keep cars happy, suburban developers widen streets to allow for ample parking space. This results in less room for planting trees and other forms of green space development in the front of homes. Subsequently, half of the frontage of a house consists of a garage door. The phrase "garage dominated architecture" seems very fitting for typical suburban residential design since the primary feature of many suburban homes is a massive garage. Alleys allow for greater green space development since both parking spaces and garages are placed on the back of homes. This planning innovation allows for additional room for landscaping and walkways along the frontage of residential areas.

Aesthetics: While alleys are often criticized for their lack of neatness, in actuality that's where all the messy stuff should be located. From trash cans, garage doors, electrical meters, and satellite dishes, the alley takes these eyesores out of public view. In new urbanism neighborhoods such as mine (Village of West Clay) alleys have become an alternative walking route for dog owners; they can walk their pets and dispose of their waste products away from children playing and parents reading papers in the front of homes. Of course, alleys need not be ugly. In older suburbs such as Baltimore's Roland Park, the rear lanes are favored as pedestrian ways between backyards, and have been known to become social centers. In Kentlands, the residents have even formed a flower-planting Alley Beautification Committee.[16]

On a more informal basis the Highlands and Crescent Hill neighborhoods of Louisville often include brick covered alleys that are lined with beautiful gardens. These brick covered back lanes lined with a hodgepodge of flower and vegetable gardens are more aesthetically appealing than the asphalt fairways cutting through America's more affluent suburbs.

Cul-de-Sac Paradise?

Despite the many advantages alleys provide for residents, most home owners report that they would rather live on a street with a cul-de-sac than within a neighborhood with alleys. These dead-end, lollipop-shaped roads seem to be an essential and often most desired part of most American suburbs. If suburbia thrives on isolation from surrounding urban areas, the cul-de-sak street may be suburbia on steroids, where only one way access and fewer homes on the block provides residents with the perception that this type of neighborhood design provides higher levels of safety and security. As discussed previously, research conducted on the relationship between neighborhood design and crime suggests that more eyes on the street, which essentially means less isolation from neighbors, actually results in lower levels of crime. Thus, fostering isolation through neighborhood design may result in greater levels criminal activity. In addition, greater access to homes through connected streets and alleys allows firefighters and police alike to respond quicker to emergencies.[17]

Historically, cul-de-sacs and curved streets go hand in hand. Both were employed within ancient cities to respond to steep topography by following undulating patterns of land. Cul-de-sacs are basically a practical response to steep and frequent valleys that do not allow streets to connect to them. Ironically this planning innovation is as common on flat land in suburbia as it is on hills. Nonetheless, curved streets and their cul-de-sac partners serve a valuable aesthetic purpose: they provide a constantly changing view as one moves through space, rather than the boring and endless vistas that can result from a long straight road. This problem, usually resulting from a gridiron street a pattern, can be avoided by modifying the grid so the continuous streets are slightly bent while maintaining their cardinal directions. In addition, cities like Savannah feature street design where differentiation exists between primary and secondary streets, and provisions are made for public open space. Essentially, all of these traditional planning strategies found within many historical neighborhoods are superior to the curve and cul-de-sac scheme in terms of both safety and aesthetics.[18]

Future of Traditional Town Planning in a Post Real Estate Crash World

America's appetite for larger homes has been growing at a steady pace since the 1970s, (see Table 4.1), but this feeding frenzy came to a screeching halt at the onset of the real estate crisis. Subsequently, average single-family home sizes declined from 2,520 square feet in 2008 to 2,480 square feet in 2009, breaking nearly 30 years of uninterrupted growth (see Table 4.1). Does this mean the era of the big home is over? Not necessarily. The last time America witnessed a decline in the average home size was during the early 1980's recession between 1979 and 1982.[19] Within four years of this real estate trough, home sizes were back above their previous peak. We see this phenomenon again in 2011, where average home size has increased to 2,480 square feet from 2,392 in 2010 (Table 4.2). In light of this insatiable demand for larger homes, it's possible that the big home may make a comeback. At this point it's difficult to determine if the recent decline in home size is a part of overall trend towards smaller homes. Current home size trends are also a reflection of the current housing market, where mortgage loans are difficult to get and higher-income households who may prefer larger homes are likely a higher proportion of homebuyers than in previous years. Nonetheless, these declines are supported by survey data from the National Association of Home Builders (NAHB) and Better Homes and Gardens (BHG), as well as paradigm shifts in policies.

Table 4.1: Mean Sq. Ft. of New Single-Family Homes Constructed in the U.S., 1973-2011 Source: *U.S. Census Bureau, 2011.*

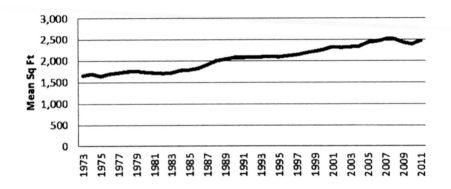

Table 4.2: Mean Sq. Ft. of New Single-Family Homes Constructed in the U.S., 2001-2011 Source: *U.S. Census Bureau, 2011*

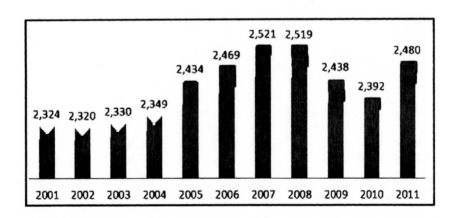

When asked about their plans for 2010, an overwhelming majority (96 percent) told NAHB they will build lower-priced models (95 percent) and smaller homes (96 percent) with a particular focus on energy savings and performance. Features such as insulated front doors, low-E windows, programmable thermostats, high performance appliances, and energy-efficient lighting were included as items most builders planned to install in their new homes. These features speak to a greater emphasis home buyers are placing on "green" construction. The results of a consumer survey by BHG show that consumers seem to be aligned with builders in their thinking. Features consumers said they most wanted in a new home included efficient HVAC systems (76 percent), Energy Star appliances (79 percent), efficient design (66 percent) and natural light (65 percent).[20]

Both short and long term policy initiatives also favor the typically smaller homes which are more likely to be a feature of traditional town planning. During housing downturns, first-time home buyers increase their share of the purchase market. First-time home buyers have one advantage over repeat buyers; they don't have to sell a home in a slow market. So, while the whole market declines, the share attributable to first-timers buying more modest homes increases and that drives home size down. In this cycle, the temporary $8,000 first-time buyer tax credit has amplified first-time buyer participation and the downward shift in size.[21]

In addition to the short term tax credit policy, longer term local and federal policies are shifting away from low density development towards their higher density counterparts. As discussed in Chapter 3, even affluent suburbs such as Carmel, IN, are finding it hard to justify the construction of costly roads and highways for newer communities with relatively few homes. For this reason, Carmel is one of many suburbs across which are making greater use of traditional planning strategies with both new residential communities, as well as within downtown revitalization and expansion plans. The trend towards traditional planning may have started within higher end communities such as Seaside and Celebration, but the federal Department of Housing and Urban Development (HUD) continues to favor the redevelopment of blighted urban areas through the initiation of new urbanism communities. The success of Louisville's Park DuValle neighborhood has served as a catalyst for many HUD supported projects. As with Park DuValle, these communities may receive federal funding or considerable tax credits for builders or new residents, but the development eventually becomes self-sustaining once most homes are occupied by new residents.

It's the Plan, Stupid!

During the 1992 presidential campaign James Carvelle cleverly deflected negative press directed at Governor Clinton by coining the phrase "it's the economy stupid!" Carvelle's ability to refocus the American public on what mattered most to them during a time of economic recession proved to be an effective campaigning strategy. A similar refocusing needs to be employed in the promotion of traditional town planning. While new urbanist communities typically include homes that are smaller and subsequently emphasize more interesting architectural amenities than their suburban counterparts, such as Italianate or Greek Revival molding, these features are merely icing on the cake. This "icing" is usually noticed first by novice admirers of traditional communities. Over the last few years that my family and I have lived in a new urbanist community, we've observed that most of our family, friends, and colleagues comment more on the designs and features of individual homes than on any other characteristic or amenity within our neighborhood. These comments range from "I love the old architecture" to the ultimate cliché "these homes are just so quaint!" That said, there is absolutely no incompatibility between traditional urbanism and modernist architecture. Anyone that has visited London has observed a host of modernist skyscrapers built alongside Baroque, Georgian, Gothic, and a variety of other traditional types of buildings. This hodgepodge of architectural styles resulting from the rebuilding of downtown London following World War II does not take away from the excitement and vitality of London's urban core- these differences in design and style enhance the downtown's aesthetic appeal. Subsequently, modernist architecture looks and works best when lining the sidewalks of traditional cities. Some truly great places-Miami's South Beach, Rome's EUR District, and Tel Aviv consist largely of modernist architecture laid out in a traditional street network.[22] These places do not suffer in any way from their modernist vocabulary, and neither do neighborhoods that combine many different eras of architecture in a true urban fabric. The unique or stately architecture may catch your eye first, but the real power lies in the traditional plan underneath the beautifully designed buildings.

The key focus of any traditional plan needs to be on the pedestrians, not cars. For this reason, one of the few times Lewis Mumford was driven towards social action during his extensive career was when Robert Moses threatened to build a four-lane highway through Washington Square, in the heart of Greenwich Village. Mumford led the fight against Moses, considering the proposed highway an act of civil vandalism. Through a succession of public petitions and pronouncements, he urged that the square be closed entirely to automobile traffic. "Washington Square," Mumford commented in a press release put out of the Committee to Close Washington Square to Traffic, "was originally used as a Potter's Field for paupers; it might now prove to be a good place to bury Mr. Moses' poverty-stricken and moribund ideas on city planning."[23] That did not happen for some time, but the square and this vital area of the Village were saved. Mayor Edward Koch, who was then a young city politician living in the Village and a member of the neighborhood action group that was fighting Moses and city hall, recalls that Mumford's contribution to this victory was decisive. Although Mumford is largely remembered as a writer, not a social activist, this event shows how committed he was throughout his life to preserving the pedestrian nature of the city. Mumford's all-consuming devotion to the perpetuation of urban areas that gave priority to "the greatest self-propelling vehicle of all," inspired a host of elected officials to develop and maintain their cities in ways that preserved the pre-automotive character of their cities. Portland's former mayor Neil Goldschmidt, who served as secretary of transportation in President Carter's administration, stated that "Portland is a better city....thanks in large part to the wisdom and foresight of Lewis Mumford."[24] As a growing number of developers, architects and elected officials are rethinking ways to build their communities in a post real estate crash world, they would also benefit from this urban writer's insights.

Notes

1. L. Mumford, *The City in History,* (New York: Harvest Books, 1961).

2. E. Blakely and M.G. Snyder, *Fortress America: Gated Communities in the United States,* (Washington D.C: Brookings Institute Press, 1997).

3. A. Duany, E. Plater-Zyberk, and J. Speck, *Suburban Nation: The Rise of Sprawl and the Decline of the American Dream,* (New York: North Point Press, 2000).

4. Duany et al, *op. cit.*

5. O. Newman, *Defensible Space: Crime Prevention Through Urban Design.* (New York: Collier Books, 1969).

6. Duany et al, *op. cit.*

7. Mayor Jim Brainard, interview by Karl Besel, 2009.

8. S. Hart and A. Spivak, *The Elephant in the Bedroom: Automobile Dependence and Denial; Impacts on the Economy and Environment,* (Pasadena, CA: New Paradigm Books, 1993).

9. Duany et al, *op. cit.*

10. Mumford, *op. cit.*

11. Duany et al, *op. cit.*

12. Brainard, *op. cit.*

13. Tom Huston, interview by Karl Besel, 2009.

14. Duany et al, *op. cit.*

15. J. Levy, *Contemporary Urban Planning (8th ed.)* (New Jersey: Pearson Prentice-Hall, 2009).

16. Duany et al, *op. cit.*

17. Levy, *op. cit.*

18. Duany et al, *op. cit.*

19. Bureau of the Census. *2011 Census Report-Summary Census Demographic Information.* Available at http://census/report.aspx.

20. Jenny Sullivan, Custom Home Magazine. "Home Prices Continue to Shrink," (Cited January 22nd, 2010). Retrieved July 5th, 2010, from http://www.customhome online.com/industry-news.

21. David Crowe, Builder: The Information Source for the Home Building Industry. "Shifting Down: Are Smaller Homes a Permanent Trend?" (Cited October 16th, 2009). Available at http://www.builderonline.com/housing-trends/shifting-down.aspx.

22. Duany et al, *op. cit.*

23. D. Miller, *Lewis Mumford: A Life,* (New York: Weidenfeld & Nicolson, 1989).

24. Goldschmidt quoted in *A Tribute to Lewis Mumford* (Cambridge, MA: Lincoln Institute of Land Policy, 1982), pp. 16, 21: interview with Perry Norton, 1988.

Chapter Five

Louisville's Historical Belles: Cherokee Triangle and Old Louisville

Karl Besel

In the minds of most outsiders, the images that are conjured up when one thinks of the Bluegrass State are horseracing, mint juleps, and coal mining. These images harken back to the pre-automotive era when high density was not one of many options for real estate development-it was the only option. As one of the oldest cities in the South, it's no surprise that Louisville became a leader in the American historical preservation movement. Its most prominent historical neighborhoods, Old Louisville and Cherokee Triangle, survived the suburban flight of the 1950s, and have subsequently managed to maintain their above average levels of real estate appreciation during the "Great Recession." This chapter provides an overview of the development and evolution of both neighborhoods, including their relationship to the new urbanism movement within the Midwest and South. In tandem with communities throughout the American heartland and South, shrewd developers took note of the above average market values found within historical neighborhoods and invested within new urbanist communities in conventionally oriented suburbs. City mayors and officials followed suit by using neo-traditional planning strategies to rebuild crime ridden inner city neighborhoods.

Cherokee Triangle

Residents of the Cherokee Triangle can attest to the fact that this historic neighborhood is far from dead. The community hosts some of main events leading up to the Kentucky Derby every spring, as well as serving as home to many of Louisville's finest restaurants. Like many other historic American communities such as Georgetown, Washington D.C., Cherokee Triangle's mixing of commercial and residential uses exhibits broad based appeal, and subsequently is home to a wide range of income and age groups. Residents enjoy the ability to walk to the Triangle's amenities, including the businesses of Bardstown road, grocery and hardware stores found adjacent to homes, as well as to Cave Hill Cemetery and the expansive Cherokee Park. After Churchill Downs, this ridge-lined urban park may be Louisville's best known amenity, developed by the famous landscape architect Frederick Olmsted (also designed New York's Central Park). In light of the Cherokee Triangle's current status as one of Louisville's most desirable neighborhoods, it's hard to believe that this historic neighborhood, where many of the city's most prominent citizens resided during the first half of the 20th Century, fell into decline during the 1950s. Its resurrection and growth during the close of the 20th Century serves as a testimony to the sustainability of mixed use, high density neighborhoods.

It didn't take long before Louisville's new city government, created in 1828, began casting yearning glances at the high ground east of the booming river town. The first major city project within this area was the development of Cave Hill Cemetery in 1848. This eastside cemetery was contoured and planted in much the same way scenic parks were being landscaped throughout large American cities; it immediately became the most prominent and popular destination point in Louisville. Former Attorney General under President Lincoln Joshua Speed and his business partner, James Henning, speculated that this land was ripe for development, and purchased 21 acres overlooking Beargrass Creek in 1967. The 1884 atlas of Louisville pinpoints the development in the Triangle to 1884.[1] The spacious Italianate, Queen Anne, and Greek Revival homes featured within the newly formed neighborhood attracted many of the city's elite, who were enticed by the "old fashioned country life" provided by this eastside development.[2] Cherokee Triangle was connected to the city's core originally by mule drawn trolleys, which were eventually replaced by their electric counterparts. A variety of commercial and community-based businesses and institutions were constructed alongside residential properties from the onset of development. These entities included churches, a retirement home, grocery stores, taverns, and other small businesses. The neighborhood continued to grow and prosper through the turn of the century, but came upon hard economic times during the Great Depression. As a result of the staggering unemployment and subsequent high foreclosure rates of the 1930s, many of the large homes in the Cherokee Triangle were converted into multifamily residences. This trend continued through the post World War II years as many city dwellers vacated older urban neighborhoods for the suburbs. Homes within the Triangle continued to be subdivided and rented. Neighborhood residents wanting to counter what they perceived as the gradual decline of their neighborhood formed the Cherokee Association in order to promote community planning, area development, as well as to "further the public aesthetic consciousnesses."[3]

This grassroots neighborhood organization determined that a strong link existed between zoning and neighborhood stability. Subsequently, the Cherokee Association organized a concerted effort to gain more zoning authority by securing designation as a historical preservation district. By the early 1970s, nearby neighborhoods such as Old Louisville and West Main Street had already acquired this federal designation. Some of the arguments leading up to the 1974 appeal to the Landmarks Commission for designation sound as timely today as it did almost 40 years ago:

> In an era of recession, inflation, pollution, and transportation problems,
> we have a workable alternative to complete suburbanization. (Lord
> 1974)

We just can't afford to waste the physical and environmental resources we have.[4]

Some of the properties designed by the architect making the latter quote (Stow Chapman) consisted of one of the more controversial philosophical questions to come before the Landmarks Commission after the Cherokee Triangle was designed. In 1975, Chapman designed three contemporary town houses for two lots within the preservation district. The modern lines and stark whiteness of these townhomes were in direct contrast to the nearby streetscape. Nonetheless, the Commission agreed with Chapman's argument that "the townhouses' lines echo the curves and turrets and tall windows of Victorian-era houses." Ultimately, the Commission deemed that contemporary structures could coexist with traditionally designed buildings within a historical neighborhood. As discussed within a previous chapter, this philosophy is also shared by new urbanist architect Andres Duany.[5]

The preservation district designation catalyzed the Cherokee Triangle into a Renaissance period, eventually leading to skyrocketing property values experienced during the 1990s. Despite the real estate crash of 2007, the neighborhood's property values remain some of the highest in the greater Louisville area, and foreclosures are almost nonexistent. Trendy restaurants which began to sprout up along the Triangle's main commercial area in the late 1970s along Bardstown Road, continue to flourish. During an era of increased economic instability and international upheaval, this historic Louisville neighborhood has managed to successfully reinvent itself into one of the most viable places to live and work in the 21st Century.

Old Louisville

Before Cherokee Triangle emerged as a "suburban" community for Louisville's most affluent citizens and members of the growing professional class, Old Louisville was the predominate neighborhood for the upper middle class and wealthy within the River City. Today this neighborhood located in the heart of Louisville is the third largest historic preservation district in the country, and the largest district containing mainly Victorian era architecture. These styles include Romanesque, Queen Anne, Italianate, and others that dominated the late 19th Century architectural scene. As early as the 1830s country estates began to appear within this area, and some of the city's earliest mansions appeared within this sparsely populated area south of downtown. Large-scale development south of Broadway did not begin until the 1870s, nearly a century after what is now Downtown Louisville was first settled. The area was initially part of three different military land grants issued in 1773, and throughout the early and mid-19th century the land passed through the hands of several speculators, meanwhile much of it was used as farmland. In its peak in the late 19th century, Old Louisville was the center of Louisville's social life, with nearly all persons listed in the *Society Directory of Louisville* having Old Louisville addresses. The directory even listed the reception days and hours of Old Louisville's leading ladies, which varied by street, such as Tuesdays on Fourth Street or Thursdays on Second.[6]

The area gradually declined in the early 1900s as the affluent moved to newer streetcar suburbs, such as Cherokee Triangle, or built estates in areas east of Louisville recently connected by railroad, such as Anchorage and Glenview. This incremental loss of wealthy and professional families throughout the first decades of the 20th Century was accelerated by America's economic collapse during the 1930s. In tandem with Cherokee Triangle, the Great Depression was a time when many of the larger homes were converted into apartments. Vacancy rates often soared during the 1930s and 1940s, leading to a drop in real estate values. Another blow to the once prosperous neighborhood was the Ohio River Flood of 1937, which caused a great number of the remaining wealthy households to move above the flood plain.[7]

The gradual abandonment of Old Louisville by the wealthy was also a reflection of changing lifestyles brought on by technology. Many homes of Old Louisville were originally built as mansions that would require several servants to maintain. Because of the relatively high wages offered by manufacturing jobs, servants which were no longer affordable to all but the wealthiest families by the mid-20th century. Interurban rail lines, and increasingly automobiles, meant that the wealthy no longer had to live so close to their businesses, and many chose to live in what had previously been summer homes in the county's east end. The lifestyle that created Old Louisville was effectively obsolete.

During the 1960s many lower income residents downtown who were displaced as a result of urban renewal moved into the newly converted apartments, especially on the north side of the neighborhood. The area was now considered drug ridden and undesirable by most Louisvillians. The very term *Old Louisville*, first becoming associated with the area in the 1940s, had mostly negative connotations initially, as historian Samuel W. Thomas put it, "In an Era where architectural styles were changing dramatically, *old* meant out of fashion."[8]

One of the first to take an active role in preserving and revitalizing Old Louisville was Courier-Journal writer J. Douglass Nunn. In 1960 he began a vigorous public information campaign concerning the area. Nunn compared it to neighborhoods like D.C.'s Georgetown and Boston's Beacon Hill. In 1961 Nunn took a leave of absence from his job and started "Restoration, Inc.," a group that restored ten homes in Old Louisville's St. James Court in 1961, spurring interest in preservation that lead many local activists moved to the area. This effort also led to the first use of the name Old Louisville in print in that year, as a reflection of the interest in preservation. With the activists' efforts the area was made into a historic preservation district in 1975.[9] The area has continued to improve, with new restaurants and shops opening and many students, and young professionals moving into the area. Property owners, who once cheaply converted the old houses to apartments, have invested more in improvements since the 1980s, and several properties have been converted into luxury condominiums. The median home value more than doubled between 1990 and 2000, increasing at a faster rate than Louisville as a whole. A variety of new restaurants and coffee shops began to appear within the neighborhood during the 1990s as Old Louisville began a destination point for college students and young professionals. These improvements and subsequent rising property values have led to a displacement of some of the community's lower income residents, causing some to criticize revitalization efforts for fostering gentrification. Nonetheless, most of the city's residents have welcomed the improvements and related commercial investments within Old Louisville which have coincided with lower crime rates in general.[10] Its close proximity to the University of Louisville and Downtown Louisville continue to serve as catalysts for both residential and small business growth.

Community Action Leading to Investment

Both of these historic neighborhoods have endured the roller coaster ride of urban neighborhood maturation. In both cases, local activists successfully organized their neighbors and community leaders to foster the right conditions for revitalization to occur. These grassroots campaigns typically started as vehicles for securing designation as a historic preservation neighborhood. This designation served as a catalyst for a number of positive byproducts, including residential and commercial investments, community festivals, as well as a general rise in property values. A recent study conducted by Gilderbloom et al (2008) shows that other historic neighborhoods within Louisville have also reaped the rewards which result from their status as historic communities. This study of 10 census tracts located within the greater Louisville area showed that the median property value increase in historic districts was 58 percent between 2000 and 2006; the appreciation rate within comparable non-historic neighborhoods within Louisville was only 32 percent.[11] The higher rates of real estate appreciation exhibited by these historical Louisville neighborhoods have been mirrored by preservation districts throughout Indiana. Economist Donovan Rypkema (1997) showed that five Indiana neighborhoods protected by local historic zoning ordinances witnessed an overall higher property appreciation, compared to similar unprotected neighborhoods.[12] Subsequent studies conducted by Rypkema (2006) and Florida (2002) have demonstrated that historic preservation practices have been a contributing factor to new capital flowing into older cities. These studies, which have been replicated with similar results in a number of metropolitan, suburban and rural settings, show the powerful relationship between preservation and economic development.[13] While the first new urbanist developments within Florida and the Eastern coastline were designed in order to foster a better quality of life than what was being offered by suburban sprawl, developers of neotraditional communities over the last 10 years have been looking primarily at gaining a return on their investment. Interviews conducted as a part of this book with the developers of new urbanist communities ranging from suburban development projects such as Norton

Commons (Louisville area) and Village of West Clay (Indianapolis area) to redevelopment projects (Park DuValle and Liberty Green (Louisville) revealed that they perceived that significant market demand existed for traditionally designed communities. These developers, as well as key city officials, often referenced the aforementioned studies as evidence that a large number of city dwellers and suburbanites alike preferred traditional development to conventional suburban strategies.

Environmental Reasons for Preserving Historic Neighborhoods

Most of chapters contained in this book provide evidence that traditional town planning is more sustainable than conventional suburban development on economic grounds. During an era of record breaking unemployment and underemployment, researchers must place the economic argument for their ideas front and center, unless they wish their work to be published only in obscure journals. Nonetheless, sustainability is about more than just providing the basic necessities of life, such as food, shelter, education, jobs, transportation, and safety in the short term. As a society we must also seek to foster the best strategies for sustaining future generations. This dimension of sustainable development is typically viewed as environmentalism. In terms of land use, energy consumption, and work commutes, historic neighborhoods are more environmentally sustainable than typical suburban communities.

Low density suburban tracks devour land in a fashion similar to that of a gas guzzling Hummer. Conventional suburban growth consumes at least four times the land area per family than their urban counterparts. Subsequently, a typical suburban household consumes three times the amount of energy per household, when compared with homes found within traditionally planned neighborhoods. The relatively smaller homes, in tandem with smaller lot sizes, found within historic districts, are less land and energy intensive than most suburban dwellings.[14]

Older neighborhoods and new housing have also been compared in terms of the ease of commuting from home to school, work, recreation, shopping, and public transportation. Within each of these categories, older neighborhoods are in closer proximity to work and to places for recreation and leisure. Older neighborhoods tend to be close to downtown as well as to other urban amenities, such as parks and museums. According to an American Housing Survey, 42 percent of all historic house residents were within five miles of their work, compared to 23 percent of people living in new housing constructed within the past four years.[15]

Final Thoughts on the Belles of Louisville

This examination of two historic preservation neighborhoods within the Louisville area reveals that traditional town development strategies have done more than survive-they have thrived within the 200 year old River City. Although the evolution of both Cherokee Triangle and Old Louisville is more comparable to a roller coaster ride than a trip to the moon, their flexible and adaptable design patterns continue to fuel neighborhood design innovations in the 21st Century. As members of the original "suburbs" of Louisville, the history of these neighborhoods embodies the strong and often insatiable appetite of the wealthy and professional class to move away from the urban core. This impulse was often motivated by a desire to "live a country life" while building wealth through a city-based profession. Unfortunately motivations to live within these newly developed "streetcar suburbs" also came in the form of white flight; a sinister desire to distance one's family from a growing number of African Americans who were seeking employment opportunities within Louisville's expanding manufacturing sector after the Civil War. As Louisville continued to grow and prosper as one of America's largest cities in the early 1990s, suburbs continued to develop east of the city and both Old Louisville and Cherokee Triangle began to be viewed more as "urban" neighborhoods.

Both neighborhoods experienced a renaissance period during the 1960s and 1970s when community activists organized campaigns to turn back the tide of suburban flight. Securing designation as historic preservation neighborhood catalyzed more restrictive zoning practices, along within improvements in property management by residents and business owners alike. The mixed use planning strategies which evolved over a century of mistakes and successes within both of these historic neighborhoods currently serve as models for development within nearby new urbanist projects such as Park DuValle, Liberty Green, and Norton Commons. The perpetuation of Old Louisville and Cherokee Triangle's community design strategies is found within these evolutionary descendants. The initiation and expansion of traditionally planned communities within the greater Louisville area reveals that the history of both Old Louisville and Cherokee Triangle is not a static one-it is continuing to unfold.

Notes

1. S.W. Thomas, *Cherokee Triangle: A History of the Heart of the Highlands,* (Louisville, KY: Butler Book Publishing, 2003).

2. Recollection of Edward Hobbs Hillard, interview by Grady Clay, 1958.

3. Thomas, *op. cit.*

4. A. Lord and S. Chapman, 1974. Quotes from S.W. Thomas, *Cherokee Triangle: A History of the Heart of the Highlands,* (Louisville, KY: Butler Book Publishing, 2003).

5. A. Duany, E. Plater-Zyberk, and J. Speck, *Suburban Nation: The Rise of Sprawl and the Decline of the American Dream,* (New York: North Point Press, 2000).

6. S.W. Thomas and W. Morgan, *Old Louisville: The Victorian Era,* (Louisville, KY: Courier-Journal, Louisville Times, and Data Courier, 1975).

7. Thomas and Morgan, *op. cit.*

8. Thomas and Morgan, *op. cit.*

9. Dan Bischoff, "Behind the Preservation Front," *Louisville Magazine,* January 1976, p.51

10. Price, Michael (2006). *Old Louisville by the Numbers: A Statistical Profile.* Available at http://srvr18.ud.net/downloads/olcc/Old_Louisville_May_06.ppt.

11. J. Gilderbloom, E. House, and M. Hanka, "Historic Preservation in Kentucky." Preservation Kentucky, Inc. (2007).

12. D. Rypkema. "Preservation and Property Values in Indiana." Historic Landmarks Foundation of Indiana. (1997).

13. D. Rykema. "Smart Growth, Sustainable Development and Historic Preservation." Presentation at the Bridging Boundaries-Building Great Communities Regional Smart Growth Conference, Louisville, KY, September 19th, 2006; and R. Florida, *The Rise of the Creative Class,* (New York: Basic Books, 2002).

14. Gilderbloom et. al. *op. cit.*

15. Gilderbloom et. al. *op. cit.*

Figure 1. Monumental Scale. The Temples of Karnack at Luxor were constructed during the lengthy reign of Ramses II. In contrast to the inflated figures shown here, Hellenic Greek sculptures were cut to the human measure. Photo by Karl Besel.

Figure 2. Sacred Mountain. The remains of a temple in Delphi, where "the life it contained was more significant than the container." While Delphi was the dominant cultural and religious center of the Hellenic world, it never developed a means to sustain a permanent population. As depicted here, Greek architects and engineers often built structures in rugged terrain, including along the sides of steep mountain cliffs. A combination of this treacherous topography and the Greek emphasis on democracy and individualism meant that most citizens lived within smaller cities or villages, where the rich often resided in the same neighborhoods as the poor. Many of the elements of Greek community life, including housing people of divergent incomes within the same neighborhood, continues to influence the builders of 21st Century new urbanism communities. Photo by Karl Besel.

Figure 3. Old Symbols Die Hard: Obelisk outside of
Luxor, Temples of Karnak. Mumford observed that
ancient symbols dating back to the Neolithic Era often reemerged in a similar form within the first cities,
and persevere into our own time. Neolithic villagers
within Africa and Europe probably built obelisks for
use as sundials to indicate festival dates. Ancient
Egyptians constructed obelisks as cult symbols to the
sun god. Obelisks of colossal size were first raised
in the XII dynasty; the upper picture features one of
the few obelisks standing in Egypt today. Several of
these ancient Egyptian symbols have been re-erected
elsewhere, such as Cleopatra's Needles in London
and New York. In the United States, the Washington
Monument, a large obelisk in the center of the nation's capital, remains one of our most prominent
American symbols. Photo by Ashley Besel.

Figure 4. Old Symbols Die Hard: Obelisk in Village of West Clay. This photo features an obelisk on a smaller scale built at the beginning of the 21st Century in the Village of West Clay, Carmel, IN. Mumford's writing about urban symbols as powerful archetypes that united city dwellers was influenced by the work of the Swiss psychiatrist Carl Jung, the founder of analytical psychology. Photo by Karl Besel.

Figure 5. Narrow Streets, Lined with Sidewalks. Seaside, Florida. Photo by Karl Besel.

Figure 6. Walkways on Steroids. Seaside, Florida. Photo by Karl Besel.

Figure 7. Nice Frontage! Cherokee Triangle, Louisville, Kentucky. Photo by Karl Besel.

Figure 8. Don't Believe the Hype about Alleys. While alleys have received a bad rap for being dangerous places, the opposite is probably true. This alley is a part of the Park Du-Valle Neighborhood on the westside of Louisville. Crime rates have actually decreased significantly within this area following the demolition of two housing projects and the subsequent construction of a new urbanism community which features a number of intentional ways of putting more "eyes on the street," including the incorporation of alleys. Alleys also provide police officers and firefighters alike with greater and quicker access to homes. Photo by Karl Besel.

Figure 9. Garage Dominant Architecture. A recent survey conducted within an undisclosed Midwestern state reveals that most cars are VERY happy with this type of residential design. The human inhabitants of the tiny house adjacent to this massive garage may beg to differ. Photo by Karl Besel.

Figure 10. Alleys Need Not Be Ugly. A brick alley within the Cherokee Triangle Historical Preservation District lined with trees and other foliage. Photo by Karl Besel.

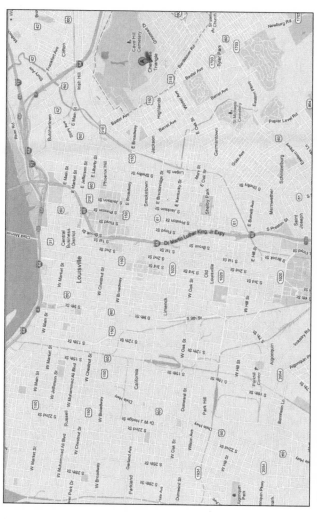

Figure 11. Cherokee Triangle and Old Louisville. Innovations in transportation led to a rapid east-ward expansion within the Derby City. Old Louisville, one of the first neighborhoods developed to house the city's professional class, is depicted in the center of this map, just west of Interstate 65. The widespread use of electric trolleys at the turn of the 20th century allowed businessmen such as Joshua Speed to develop new residential communities east of the central business district. Cherokee Triangle (labeled as "A") quickly became a trendy neighborhood for the educated and relatively affluent in the early 1900s. Cherokee Triangle's growth and vibrancy led to Old Louisville's gradual decline and decay. Source: 2012 Google.

Figure 12. Before and After: Cotter and Lang Housing Projects. This photo shows the Cotter and Lang Housing Projects before demolition in the 1990s when the Park Du-Valle neighborhood exhibited the highest crime rate in Kentucky. Photo by Community Builders.

Figure 13. Before and After: Park DuValle Neighborhood. This photo depicts a neighborhood view of the Villages of Park DuValle after the completion of this new urbanist redevelopment project. Photo by Community Builders.

Figure 14. More Similar than Different: Park DuValle. Photo by Community Builders.

Figure 15. More Similar than Different: Village of West Clay. Photo by Karl Besel.

Figure 16. Main Entrance to Haile Plantation. Photo by Muthusami Kumaran.

Figure 17. Tioga Town Center and Entrance to the Town of Tioga. Photo by Muthusami Kumaran.

Figure 18. New Urbana Commercial District. Photo by John Vick.

Figure 19. New Urbana Streetscape. Photo by John Vick.

Figure 20. Southwood Estate Streetscape. Photo by John Vick.

Chapter Six

A Tale of Two Villages: Park DuValle and West Clay

Karl Besel and Hervil Cherubin

Most people are familiar with the beginning sentence of Dicken's classic, *A Tale of Two Cities*. This contradictory first sentence (It was the best of times, it was the worst of times) is followed by other paradoxical sentences that speak to the scientific and political innovations and advancements, as well as the inhumanity and deprivation of the Age of Enlightenment, especially during the French Revolution[1]. An opening paragraph on American neighborhood development (and I use that term loosely) over the past 50 years could easily mimic Dicken's literary style. The best and brightest architects and planners believed well designed buildings could transform individuals so they demolished entire city blocks and constructed housing projects such as Pruitt Igoe and Cabrini Green[2]. We know how that turned out. As the Baby Boom generation prepared to retire, developers increased the average size of the American home to unprecedented levels. The federal government promised the American dream of homeownership to millions of Americans, only to displace these individuals after the demise of Freddie Mac and Fannie Mae. The United States has been the richest and most powerful country on the globe since the end of World War II, but byproducts of this prosperity have been rampant sprawl, pollution, and traffic congestion. Fortunately a phoenix has been able to rise up from the ashes of failed housing policy, unscrupulous developers, and predatory mortgage lenders. As discussed in Chapter 3, market demand for new urbanism housing continues to grow within suburban America. In addition, the federal agencies such as the U.S. Department of Housing and Urban Development (HUD) have supported the use of traditional town planning principles to revitalize a number of America's most blighted neighborhoods. In light of this mixed history of neighborhood development within the U.S., I am reminded of the famous Winston Churchhill quote, "America finally does the right thing after exhausting all other possibilities."

While most articles published on new urbanism have merely offered this planning scheme as an alternative to conventional suburban development (i.e., Plas and Lewis, 1996; Harvey, 1997; Poticha, 2000a, 2000b) some recent publications have focused on inner city new urbanism (i.e., Larsen, 2005; Garde, 2006; White and Ellis, 2007). This dearth of scholarly work on inner city new urbanism may be attributed to the fairly recent attention being paid to traditional town planning strategies by public housing officials. Subsequently, these planning strategies were not emphasized by the federal government until former HUD secretary Henry Cisneros signed the Charter of the New Urbanism in 1996. Nonetheless, since Cisneros embraced new urbanism through the signing of this charter, as well as initiating the "Homeownership Zones" program which offered grants and loans to cities for redevelopment based on new urbanist principles, a relatively large number of projects have been completed or are under construction throughout the U.S.[3] In its December 2002 survey of new urbanist projects (Steuteville, 2002), New Urban News identified 472 neighborhood-scale projects either built, under construction, or in planning in the U.S. Fifty-seven percent (269) were greenfield projects and 43% (204) were infill developments, including 25 brownfield reuses.[4] Despite the rapid speed at which new urbanism communities are being built throughout urban America, many urban planning critics seem to be unaware of these initiatives.[5]

This case study seeks to highlight how traditional planning strategies are being employed within both the inner city and suburbs. The inner city community (Park DuValle, Louisville) constitutes an infill development project; this new urbanist project was completed over ten years was built on the site of two former housing projects. This redevelopment project was one of the first of its kind in America, and subsequently represents a reversal in federal public housing strategies. Jane Jacobs was one of the fiercest critics of many of the urban renewal schemes of the 1950s and 60s, especially the destruction of "crime ridden slums" so that seemingly more humane and safer housing projects could be constructed. The Villages of Park DuValle, while more intentionally planned than many inner city neighborhoods at the beginning of the 20th Century, still resembles most pre-automotive city neighborhoods with its alleys, Greek Revival architecture, and accessible community businesses. In essence, Park DuValle was the type of city neighborhood development favored by Jacobs, and the significantly lower crime rates exhibited since the construction of this community seem to support her theories on what types of neighborhoods foster greater levels of safety and cohesiveness. Within this chapter Park DuValle is compared and contrasted with a suburban counterpart, the Village of West Clay, located outside of Indianapolis in Carmel, Indiana. Both communities were the first of their kind in their respective states, in addition to being two of the first new urbanism developments built within the Midwest.[6] The following analysis of these communities a decade after their inception seeks to highlight not only differences between urban infill development and new urbanism within a suburban community, but also to discuss common convergent themes within both inner city and suburban development.

The Villages of Park DuValle

During an interview with Mayor Jerry Abramson of Louisville in the fall of 2009, I found out as much about the latest new urbanist project within Kentucky's largest metropolitan area as I did Park DuValle. "We're making Liberty Green more urban with more condos" than Park DuValle, stated the longest serving mayor in Louisville's history. Mayor Abramson's enthusiasm for this latest infill project which stands on the site of the former Clarksdale Housing Project probably stems from the huge success of the debut new urbanist project within the Derby City. Although Louisville and many other cities throughout the U.S. are currently trying to capitalize on the achievements of Park DuValle by embarking on similar redevelopment strategies, success was anything but guaranteed when the idea was initially proposed in the early 1990's. When Mayor Abramson in tandem with city officials applied for federal empowerment zone funding to tear down the Cotter and Lang housing projects in order to redevelop the neighborhood as a new urbanist community, their proposal was rejected. "Fortunately the mayor was able to hold key people together" who were a part of the Empowerment Zone proposal, according to Vice President of Development Willie Jones.[7] Jones is employed by Baltimore based nonprofit Community Builders which served as the housing and commercial development company for The Villages of Park DuValle. These key stakeholders included administrators from a local community development bank, the Louisville Housing Authority, as well as local leaders and Westside residents. When the opportunity came in 1994 to apply for other funding through the Enterprise Zone program, the city was able to secure these funds, as well as receiving financial support from HUD's new HOPE VI program. Jones attributes Mayor Abramson's ability to build consensus amongst a divergent group of area stakeholders, the community development bank's initial success in spurring economic activity, and the "grand vision" effectively cast by the city's planning group as key component in the success of Park DuValle. "An awful lot of work had already been done" before Community Builders was awarded the contract to redevelop this Westside neighborhood which exhibited the highest crime rates within Kentucky in 1990.

While the original Park DuValle redevelopment proposal was rejected by HUD, by the late 1990s the City of Louisville and Community Builders had successfully secured financing from a variety of federal and local funders. The approximately $220 million in funding support for The Villages of Park included but was not limited to 31.4 million from the Louisville Metro Housing Authority, $37.5 million in the form of equity tax credits, $56.3 million debt financing, $40 million from HUD/HOPE VI grants, as well as 10 million secured for infrastructure improvements from the City of Louisville.[8] In addition to these revenue sources, the mayor negotiated a direct appropriation from Secretary Cisneros for the project. According to Executive Director of the Louisville Metro Housing Authority Tim Barry, "You could never do this today. Jerry was able to do this for a couple of reasons. First, HUD recognized we had an exciting, viable development idea that was different from anything they had ever seen. Secondly, the mayor just wore them down," quipped Barry. Essentially half of the funds for the project came from governmental sources, and the remaining half were received in the form of private sector tax credits.[9]

The redevelopment of the Park DuValle neighborhood consisted of four distinct phases. The initial phase included the construction of single family homes lined with alleys and narrow streets, as well as commercial development. Park DuValle's first businesses included a wide variety of service and retail establishments, such as a restaurant, beauty shop, H and R Block, a retirement center, as well as a nonprofit health center. Most of these initial businesses were built within the town center, with the most viable establishments being "the service agencies rather the retail ones," according to Community Builder's Vice President Jones. "I would have to say the least successful part of this total revitalization was our ability to activate a commercial zone with a lot of retail capacity. The service industries, such as insurance companies, seem to be to remain viable, especially within the town center," according to Jones. While service oriented business were more likely to locate within the town center than retail oriented ones, some of the service agencies Community Builders attempted to bring to Park DuValle didn't respond well to the community's new urbanism plan. "This insurance company was interested in opening up a shop within the town center but couldn't get around the lack of parking that often goes along with new urbanism," quipped Jones. Community Builders Vice President is quick to state "the residential side of developing Park DuValle was easier and went better than the commercial side."[10]

The substantial demographic changes included lower crime rates, as well as increases in median family incomes once both current neighborhood residents and homebuyers from outside of the community began to move into the redeveloped city blocks. When the Cotter and Lang housing projects stood within the Park DuValle neighborhood, 1,116 rental units were available to lower income residents. With the establishment of the Villages of Park DuValle, 613 newly constructed rental units were available to mixed-income residents.[11] While the newly created Villages of Park DuValle had to demonstrate for federal reporting purposes that at least one third of the available housing was available for lower income residents, the new urbanist model appealed to many middle class African American families. Between 1990 and 2008 the median family income within the Park DuValle area had risen from $5,269 to $29,849. Although the neighborhood was transformed from one populated by individuals receiving public assistance to a mixed income community, the neighborhood remains predominately African American. Approximately 98 percent of Park DuValle's citizens were African American in 1990; this figure remains virtually unchanged today.[12]

The Village of West Clay

As ground was being broken on the innovative yet risky Park DuValle infill redevelopment project, developers George Sweet and Tom Huston had their eye on the cornfields within West Clay Township for a similar new urbanism community. The setting for the Village of West Clay couldn't be more different than Park DuValle, demographically speaking. Carmel, Indiana, the proposed site for the Village of West Clay, is a predominately Caucasian bedroom community of Indianapolis exhibiting one of the highest median family incomes within the state. On the other hand, Park DuValle's residents are predominately African American, and the neighborhood exhibited one of the lowest median incomes within Louisville before this new urbanist project was completed. Nonetheless, Sweet and Huston's development company, Brenwick, also experienced their share of rejection when their "radical" proposal was presented to the planning commission, according to Brenwick's former Director of Operations Jose Kruetz. "They flat out rejected our proposal the first time. Normally it takes six months to get approval to zone a project....it took us two years to get approval for the Village of West Clay," according to Kruetz.[13] In order to comprehend why a local planning commission would reject a development project that seemed to possess considerable merits, one needs to understand the member selection process for local planning commissions, as well as their priorities. Members are selected from the local community, and subsequently embrace the economic and political goals of long standing members of the region. Economically, the commission's priorities include maximizing real estate appreciation levels for current residents; this objective has a tendency to make commission members apprehensive about development proposals that are significantly different from the status quo. In addition, the smaller lot sizes were connoted with "being cheap" and would drive down existing market rates for real estate, according to developer Tom Huston. Politically, Brenwick was up against a "West Clay Township vs. City of Carmel mentality," according to Carmel's city planner Mike Hollibaugh.[14] When plans for building the Village of West Clay were being proposed to the planning commission and city officials during the late 1990s, commercial infrastructure and subdivisions had been developed for decades around the eastside's turn of the century downtown area. In contrast with the mix of older smaller homes, business district, and aging suburban tracts that epitomize Carmel's eastside, the suburb's westside remained fairly undeveloped, even rural. "People often selected to live west of Highway 31 in Carmel because they could reside on at least an acre and a half of land. They wanted the area to remain low density with large homes, lots, and farms.........some local residents still staunchly oppose the Village of West Clay," according to Hollibaugh. In light of the fierce objections some Westside residents mounted against Brenwick's proposed high density community, the development company was fortunate to find an ally in Carmel's mayor. "The project wouldn't exist if it wasn't for the vision of Brainard and his planning staff," according to Brenwick developer Tom Huston. Brenwick's controversial development plan ultimately prevailed after galvanizing support from city officials. As demonstrated in Table 6.1, low density housing was "blended" with the Village Core Area in order to mitigate some of the local resistance to a high density community. These lower density areas around the perimeter serve as a buffer between sparsely populated west Carmel neighborhoods and the mixed use housing found within most of the Village. While this proposed buffer zone of lower density homes around the boarder of the neighborhood was a factor in the approval process, one of the main reasons the planning commission ultimately approved the new urbanist community related to increased levels of safety. "We presented information to the planning commission about how the average speed limit within most suburban neighborhoods designed with curvilinear streets is between 30-50 miles per hour. Within the Village most of the streets would be linear, and as a result most cars would drive under 20 miles per hour," according to Brenwick's former director of operations.[15] After zoning for the Village of West Clay was approved and new residents began to build their Greek Revival, Italianate, and Federalist style homes, Brenwick's developers even seemed surprised at how quickly real estate within the Village began to appreciate. Other developers within the area took notice of the above average appreciation levels residents within the Village of West Clay were enjoying, and subsequently broke ground on a number of similar high density communities around Carmel, as well as within the neighboring northside suburb of Zionsville.[16] It appeared that even within the quintessentially American suburb of Carmel, Indiana, that new urbanism had appeal, if not pizzazz.

Table 6.1: Density Ratings in the Village of West Clay and West Carmel

Neighborhood	Over 4.0	3.99-2.0	1.99-1.0	Less than 1.0
	Density Ratings			
Stanford Park (townhomes)	7.16			
Village of West Clay (core area)	**4.50**			
Stanford Park		3.21		
Village of West Clay		**2.54**		
Heather Knoll			1.99	
Trails of Hayden Run			1.63	
Hayden Run			1.56	
Aberdeen Bend			1.36	
Lakes at Towne Road			1.34	
Wexley Chase			1.33	
Claridge Farms			1.32	
Clay Spring Meadows			1.30	
High Grove			1.28	
Laurel Lakes			1.22	
Village of Towne Pointe				.93
Crossfields				.66
Estates of West Clay				.55

Source: *City of Carmel, 2010*

Similarities between the Villages

Former HUD Secretary Henry Cisneros stated at a 2009 Brookings Institution presentation that "places that were sink holes for anything positive in the city, are replaced with communities that are frequently indistinguishable from the attractive private investment that's now occurring in the surrounding neighborhoods."[17] A drive through both of these new urbanist neighborhoods reveals that the former HUD secretary's words are more than just rhetoric; they are reality as depicted within the pictures below. Both of these pictures show common features of new urbanism being manifested within the inner city and suburbs. In both cases lots are relatively small and lined with sidewalks in the front and alleys in the back. Architecture, in tandem with the neighborhood plan, is also traditional. Greek Revival architecture is the predominant style of choice for the street blocks depicted below, but Craftsman and Federalist style architecture also appear within both neighborhoods. The Village of West Clay contains some of the more costly traditional home designs, such as Italianate, but even these homes are often adjacent to a Greek Revival or Federalist style homes, consistent with the wide mix of housing available within both communities. The range of home designs and subsequent home prices available within Park DuValle is a key component of new urbanism, and finds its inspiration within Louisville's historic neighborhoods, such as the River City's primary turn of the century downtown historical preservation district called Old Louisville. "I think there's no better example of a sustainable urban neighborhood than Old Louisville," according to Louisville's housing director.[18] There are people from all incomes living in these neighborhoods, and always have been." In tandem with city blocks with the Washington D.C.'s Georgetown neighborhood, Old Louisville is able to attract a wide range of incomes, from college students to doctors and attorneys. Inspirations for the neighborhoods plans and architectural styles for the Village of West Clay were also found within historic neighborhoods within Indiana, as well as within the South. Developer Tom Huston made a point of taking his team of builders to Savannah, Georgia, and Charleston, South Carolina "so they could see how they dealt with both privacy and (income) diversity within 19th Century communities."[19] In addition to being influenced by the plans and designs of these historic cities, smaller historic towns within Indiana such as Madison, Crawfordsville, and Zionsville also served as inspirations for West Clay.[20] Both Park DuValle and West Clay have demonstrated that like the historic neighborhoods which came before them, significant demand does exist for mixed income developments. One hundred families that formerly lived within the Cotter and Lang housing projects returned to the Villages of Park DuValle when construction was completed. The apartments where they now reside are situated amongst a diverse collection of single family homes with market values between 130,000 to almost $300,000. Within a little more than a decade the Park DuValle neighborhood seems to have been transformed from a "warehouse for the poor" to a community capable of sustaining a broad range of incomes.

Louisville residents that make a point of keeping up with the local news are probably not surprised to hear about Park DuValle mixed income neighborhoods. Mayor Abramson perceived Park DuValle as one of his key successes, and subsequently discussed the new urbanism community while campaigning. In contrast with Park DuValle, the Village of West Clay is often perceived, even amongst Carmel residents, as being somewhat elitist. This reputation may result from some high profile residents within the Village, including a member of the Simon Family, as well as some local sports celebrities. "Locals often don't realize the variety of properties available within the Village. You have everything from $60,000 condos to 3 million dollar homes. Family incomes are all over the place because of this range of housing available — you won't find that anywhere else in Carmel," according to local realtor Jack Goreki.[21] The sprawling Italianate and Mediterranean style homes that line West Clay's Broad Street may have fueled the impression of elitism within West Clay, but the more modest townhomes have been more popular than Brenwick ever imagined. "Townhomes were not included in the original plan, but they were so successful that we developed them on the Westside of the Village. We never compromised on neighborhood design or architecture, but we're not a nonprofit venture..... There was definite market demand for this type of housing, and we responded to the market," according to Brenwick Developer Tom Huston.[22]

In addition to sharing commonalities with regard to neighborhood plans, designs, and mixed income housing, both communities also struggled in attracting and sustaining a vibrant commercial sector. In turn, the developers of both Park DuValle and the Village of West both reported that "the commercial development side was much harder than the residential side." Some shared predicaments in fostering a sustainable collection of neighborhood businesses include lack of visibility and subsequent dependence upon neighborhood residents for business. In light of these dilemmas, some establishments within both neighborhoods have decided to locate their businesses on the main fairways bordering their respective communities. Community Builders Vice President Jones states that while some retail businesses have already been forced to close within Park DuValle, several restaurants and other agencies have opened along the highway leading to the neighborhood. "I was very disappointed with retail development within the village center area of Park DuValle, but I think the development of our residential community revitalized an abandoned shopping complex on 35th Street, down the block from Park DuValle" stated Jones. This complex went from being completely desolate to becoming home to a number of fast food restaurants and government agencies. Essentially, Park DuValle catalyzed business development within this abandoned commercial site. While restaurants, grocery stories, and retail oriented have found that they often need to maximize their visibility, service oriented agencies, such as insurance agents, dentist offices, and financial/accounting firms have done well within both communities.[23]

A final area that the two communities share consists of their intergenerational nature. Both Park DuValle and West Clay include amongst residential developments schools as well as retirement homes. The cradle to grave amenities found within these new urbanism communities typically resided within most small towns and urbanized neighborhoods a century ago, but are noticeably absent from America's suburbs. While urban neighborhoods continue to manifest more diverse age demographics than their suburban counterparts, the increase in the number of single adults and empty nesters, primarily as a result of young people delaying marriage, as well as the aging of the baby boomers, is fostering a radical makeover outside of America's cities- the suburbs are looking just as intergenerational as urban neighborhoods! Subsequently, a recent housing market analysis report conducted for the City of Carmel predicts that household heads between the ages of 55 and 64 will be the fastest growing market segment within Clay Township-the area exhibiting the most rapid growth pattern within

Carmel. These empty nester households are expected to account for between 45 to 50 percent of the net growth within Carmel's market over the next five years. This report also shows that while less than 10 percent of the demand for new sales in a typical Clay Township development comes from singles and couples without children, between 10 to 15 percent of the new sales activity at the Village of West Clay comes from this demographic.[24] The small and narrow lot Village section (shown in the picture above) is especially appealing to singles and couples without children. Essentially, the intergenerational amenities and wide range of housing available within the Village of Clay will probably provide this new urbanism community with a competitive advantage over other developments within the township. Carmel is not alone in noticing a change in the demographic makeup of their neighborhoods-Richard Florida (2002) and many other scholars have made similar observations about America's changing suburbs, based mainly on census data projections.[25] Suburbs that continue to appeal solely to young families with children are ignoring these demographic trends, and therefore risk their own extinction.

Differences

While both Park DuValle and the Village of West Clay both struggled more with the commercial side of development more than the residential side, the two communities differ with the types of businesses which have sustained their operations for at least five years. The suburban development is able to support a relatively high number of independently owned businesses which cater to higher income demographic. In contrast, the businesses within or surrounding Park DuValle are primarily financial or fast food service oriented chains, such as H and R Block, Wendy's, and Kentucky Fried Chicken. Subsequently, Park DuValle's developer seemed very enthusiastic about the initiation of these establishments; West Clay has been able to induce and retain a wide variety of innovative small businesses that cannot be found anywhere else in Carmel. The few chains that appear within West Clay consist of a couple of banks, and a CVS. The few chains that call West Clay home appear remarkably different from most of their counterparts; the community's CVS looks more like a small town movie theater than a drug store with its Art Deco style architecture. Most of these differences in the composition of the commercial sector within the two developments are a function of median family incomes. In contrast to West Clay Township's median family income of approximately $170,000, Park DuValle's average family income is around $30,000.[26] The substantially higher amount of disposable income found within West Clay allows the suburban community to support a much wider variety of niche businesses and high end stores. Along with the broader selection of agencies and businesses, exterior building materials within West Clay include hearty plank siding, brick, and stucco. Park DuValle homes use primarily vinyl siding for residential properties.

Outside of these somewhat obvious and superficial differences, probably the main distinction between inner city and suburban developments entails differences with regard to population density. Table 6.1 shows that the "Core Area" of the Village of West Clay exhibits almost triple the density rating when compared to other developments on the Westside of Carmel, and the overall density rating is approximately double that of other communities within the township. The only development which possesses a higher density rating than West Clay is Stanford Park, which consists primarily of townhomes and subsequently does not include single family homes. In contrast to higher than average density rating found within West Clay, the density fell dramatically within the Park DuValle neighborhood after its housing projects were demolished and the current new urbanism development was populated. The 125 acre neighborhood went from a total population of 4,347 to 1,355 from 1990 to 2008. Subsequently, the number of families dropped from 1,086 to 384, in tandem with the number of households falling from 1,216 to 543 during the same time period.[27] This reduction in Park DuValle's neighborhood density has resulted in some criticism that the new urbanist community fueled gentrification. Community activists often fairly accused developers and city officials of gentrifying neighborhoods during the 1960s when displaced tenants had no place to go in the absence of a safety net. Indeed, the challenge faced by most center cities today is not to provide affordable housing, which they typically supply at alarming ratios through public subsidies, but to create a market for the middle class. In light of Park DuValle's success in attracting a critical mass of middle class families to reside within its single family homes, and subsequently raising the median family income within the neighborhood, the community has flourished as a result. After all, cities cannot remain vibrant and dynamic without taxpaying residents.[28]

Conclusion

This tale of two communities shows how flexible and adaptable traditional town planning is within two distinct settings. While redevelopment neighborhoods such as Park DuValle cannot possibly support a wide variety of independently owned businesses, they can include traditional neighborhood design and architectural styles. This case study also indicates that in light of demographic trends, demand for homes within new urbanist style neighborhoods will probably continue to remain high well into the 21st Century. If anything, suburban developers that cater solely to young families through single use neighborhood design will find themselves at a competitive disadvantage. The success of communities such as Park DuValle and West Clay, as evidenced by increased median family incomes and market demand respectively, has already catalyzed the initiation of similar developments within their respective areas. Liberty Green seeks to build upon the achievements of Park DuValle by providing a similar mix of condos, apartments, and single family homes adjacent to the University of Louisville Medical School, and downtown amenities. Like Park DuValle, Liberty Green is being constructed on the site of a former housing project. In contrast to this redevelopment project, the new urbanist communities that have been initiated on the fringe of Indianapolis's northside are more varied. Some appear very much like conventional suburbs, possessing limited or no alleys, wide streets, and few businesses. Others may exhibit higher density ratings than even West Clay in light of a greater emphasis being placed on townhome development. Still others have been more aggressive about fostering a dynamic commercial sector. While new urbanism manifests itself within a variety of planning strategies, the appetite for this type of neighborhood design is clear. As both the inner city and suburbs respond to the demand for traditional town planning within metropolitan areas such as Indianapolis and Louisville, it's looking more like we're going to back to the future.

Notes

1. C. Dickens, *A Tale of Two Cities,* (London: Oxford University Press).

2. A. Duany, E. Plater-Zyberk, and J. Speck, *Suburban Nation: The Rise of Sprawl and the Decline of the American Dream,* (New York: North Point Press, 2000).

3. Ajay Garde, "Designing and Developing New Urbanist Projects in the United States: Insights and Implications," *Journal of Urban Design,* Vol. 11, No. 1, (2006): 33-54.

4. New Urbanism News (n.d.) Available at http://www.newurbanismnews.com/, accessed December 15th, 2004.

5. Stacey White and Cliff Ellis, "Sustainability, the Environment, and New Urbanism: An Assessment and Agenda for Research," *Journal of Architectural and Planning Research,* Vol. 24, No. 2 (2007): 125-142.

6. Mayor Jerry Abramson and Tom Huston, interviews by Dr. Karl Besel, 2009.

7. Vice President of Development Willie Jones, interview by Dr. Karl Besel, 2009.

8. Executive Director of the Louisville Metro Housing Authority Tim Barry, interview by Dr. Hervil Cherubin, 2010.

9. Tim Barry, *op. cit.*

10. Willie Jones, *op. cit.*

11. Tim Barry, *op. cit.*

12. Federal Financial Institutions Examination Council, *2010 Census Reports-Summary Census Demographic Information.* Available at http://www.ffiec.gov/Geocode/CensusDemo.aspx.

13. Former Brenwick Director of Development Jose Kruetz, interview by Dr. Karl Besel, 2009.

14. City of Carmel Planner Mike Hollibaugh, interview by Dr. Karl Besel, 2009.

15. Jose Kruetz, *op. cit.*

16. Realtor Jack Gorecki, interview by Dr. Karl Besel, 2009.

17. Former Secretaries, U.S. Department of Housing and Urban Development (HUD) Henry Cisneros and Shawn Donovan, *From Despair to Hope: Two HUD Secretaries on Urban Revitalization and Opportunity.* The Brookings Institution. Conference Presentation on July 14th, 2009, Washington D.C.

18. Tim Barry, *op. cit.*

19. Brenwick Developer Tom Huston, interview by Dr. Karl Besel, 2009.

20. Jose Kruetz, *op. cit.*

21. Jack Gorecki, *op. cit.*

22. Tom Huston, *op. cit.*

23. Tom Huston and Willie Jones *op. cit.*

24. *Market Segments: Potential Demand and Product Opportunities.* Report Prepared for the City of Carmel by Jackson Research and Consulting, June, 2009.

25. R. Florida, *Suburban Nation: The Rise of the Creative Class* (New York: Basic Books, 2002).

26. Federal Financial Institutions Examination Council, *op. cit.*

27. Tim Barry and Willie Jones, *op. cit.*

28. According to Duany et. al (2000), there is a form of gentrification that should always be fought: government-imposed speculative gentrification, in which cities attempt to stimulate rebuilding downtown areas by raising their zoning capacity. This technique results in an increased tax assessment, which more often than not forces existing residents and businesses to depart. Meanwhile, the resulting higher land values actually end up impeding development, since the large-scale projects suggested by the new zoning present a risk that often can be undertaken only by the large developer.

Chapter Seven

New Urbanism in a University Town: The Case of Gainesville and the University of Florida

Muthusami Kumaran, Molly Moon, and Kimberly Ambayec

Universities as Agents of Urbanization

Historically, universities and their host urban centers have developed symbiotic relationships where the urban host contributed to the growth of universities and the universities, in turn, contributed to the economic and physical vitality of the host cities[1]. This inherent inter-dependence between the host cities and universities has also resulted in numerous other mutual benefits.

Large universities represent vast resources that can transform surrounding urban and suburban communities. The revenues they receive from governments, tuition fees, extramural grants and contracts make these universities major economic entities. As large players in local economies, they supply a great number of jobs, contracts to suppliers and vendors, and other investment opportunities. They attract large and diversified revenue bases from financial institutions (for banking, mortgage, insurance, etc.), retail businesses (supplies, consumer and food outlets), startup high-tech companies (that tap into university based research), and student housing facilities[2].

In addition to economic development, another area of urban development that is more visible due to the presence of universities is residential development. The concentration of university programs, research activities, and facilities in an urban location has a strong influence on land use, neighborhood revitalization and new residential developments. However, universities need not commit large resources to attract development to their physical environments. These development projects are financed, for the most part, by private investors.[3]

Universities have also played vital roles in environmental and physical changes that have resolved urban issues and promoted positive residential and community images. In return, these positive city images have impacted the universities by enhancing their recruitment of quality students, faculty, and staff. With their cadres of faculty, researchers, paraprofessionals, and other employees, larger universities command considerable share of the residential markets in surrounding urban and suburban areas. Especially, universities with medical schools and affiliated medical centers or hospitals have stronger impacts on high-end residential developments. University physicians and other medical professionals, who have higher levels of disposable income, tend to live in exclusive residential areas with better amenities.

Urban centers dominated by economic and physical development spurred by universities have come to be known as university towns. Depending on their urban location's land availability and real estate market values, large university communities have adopted two major approaches to control sprawl and promote viable (and often vibrant) residential neighborhoods. Universities located in high density large urban areas with high real estate values have focused on redeveloping and revitalizing neighborhoods that have suffered neglect over several decades. This controlled development process often called "smart growth" emphasizes zoning, revitalizes neighborhoods to make them attractive, facilitates better transportation choices, and fosters a stronger sense of place among residents. As partners in *smart growth*, universities have played active roles in deploying their intellectual and institutional resources on their immediate environment and often contributed novel and good solutions to severe urban problems.[4] Federal government programs such as the Department of Education's University-Community Partnership program and the Department of Housing and Urban Development's Community Outreach Partnership Centers (COPC) program engaged universities to resolve and revitalize communities that were in decline.[5]

Recently, several universities located in mid-size cities with better availability of land and lower real estate values started to follow the new urbanism concepts that favored the development of residential neighborhoods and sub-divisions with improved designs that included more walking paths, community amenities, and green space. While smart growth, for the most part, focuses on redevelopment, new urbanism focuses on new development with improved land use and design elements.

Promoted by private developers and builders, new urbanism designs and developments in university towns primarily target and cater to the needs of university employees, especially faculty, physicians and other professionals. For university towns, new urbanism communities managed to produce an environment with improved physical characteristics, effective residential land use patterns, and desirable residential neighborhood amenities. As a result, more university employees with disposable income started to relocate to these communities.

Gainesville, the University Town of North Central Florida

The City of Gainesville and its Metropolitan Statistical Area, which includes Alachua County, are located in North Central Florida between two of Florida's thoroughfares, Interstate 75 and US Highway 441, at approximately equal distance from the Gulf of Mexico and the Atlantic Ocean (Gainesville Visitor and Conventional Bureau). The 2009 population estimate for the City of Gainesville was 116,616 and that of Gainesville metropolitan area was 243,574 (US Census Bureau).

Due to its topography, surrounding lakes and springs, higher level of subterranean water tables, year round rain fall, and the presence of a vast network of aquifers, Gainesville is surrounded by lush vegetation and canopies of matured trees adorned with Spanish moss. According to the University of Florida's School of Forest Resources and Conservation estimates, Gainesville's tree canopy has about 3 million trees. Gainesville had earned the status of "Tree City USA" from the National Arbor Day Foundation for 29 consecutive years since 1982 when the Foundation began its list of Tree Cities USA (National Arbor Day Foundation).

Based on the analysis of 375 metropolitan areas in the US and Canada that used more than a dozen variables, the book *Cities Ranked and Rated*, published in 2007, ranked Gainesville as the best place to live in USA. The authors of the book stated that "Gainesville, home to the University of Florida, has gained popularity among Northern migrants seeking a Florida climate and intellectual stimulation without the high prices, tourist bustle, and stigma most associated with the state."[6]

The University of Florida and Santa Fe College are two prominent educational institutions in Gainesville. The University of Florida has an annual enrollment of more than 50,000 students, making it among the largest 10 public universities in the country. Santa Fe College has an annual enrollment of about 12,000 students, making it one of the largest community colleges in the country. The history, size and impacts of the University of Florida on Gainesville are provided in the next section. Santa Fe Community College was established by the state government in 1965 to offer wide access to quality higher education. Since then, it has established programs and services to carry out its mission of educational opportunity, responsiveness to the community, economic development, and innovation in the public interest. The philosophy of the College has been, and continues to be, one of student centeredness. Student enrollment has grown rapidly. While fewer than 1,000 students enrolled when classes were first offered in September 1966, today, more than 17,000 students take classes at the college. Santa Fe College offers a variety of educational options through its seven different campus sites conveniently located throughout Alachua and Bradford counties. Santa Fe College was authorized by the State of Florida in 2009 to offer baccalaureate degrees that meet demands for specific skills needed in the economy. Santa Fe College employs almost 700 faculty members (230 full-time and 457 part-time). Support and administrative staff is comprised of 507 full-time and 46 part-time employees. The operating budget for Santa Fe College is approximately $77 million dollars. Nowadays, Santa Fe College has major economic, residential, and developmental impacts on Gainesville.

Gainesville and the University of Florida in History

The history of the University of Florida is linked directly to the historical development of Gainesville and Alachua County, Florida. Prior to the establishment of Alachua County in 1824, the Seminole Indians and Spaniards were the earliest inhabitants. When Alachua County was established, the land area stretched from the Georgia border to Charlotte Harbor and had a population of approximately 8,000 people. Today, that same area encompasses 20 different counties. Gainesville, Florida was established as the new county seat in 1860 and had a population of 223, mostly white and almost half from South Carolina. In 1925, Alachua County, Florida was established as the land size it currently is.[7]

During the Civil War, Gainesville was designated a Confederate Commissary serving as the food depot for all of central Florida. Large herds of cattle from South Florida were transported to and from the area in support of the Confederacy. After the Civil War, during reconstruction, the population of the county doubled. At the time, the black population was twice larger than the white population. At the beginning of the 20th century, the economic prosperity of the area and the tremendous building boom in Gainesville managed to offset the racial and political turmoil that was prevalent in the years that followed the Civil War.[8]

Florida's university system was reorganized during the late 1800s and early 1900s. At the time, the state was financially supporting nine different colleges in the state. Due to the large number of state supported colleges, there was much competition for students and state funds. Therefore, in 1905, the state abolished all existing institutions and consolidated universities. As a result, the Florida Female College (now Florida State University) and the University of Florida for men were created.[9]

The cities of Gainesville and Lake City competed for the University of Florida. Gainesville was awarded the university with a bid that included 517 acres west of the city for a school site, a cash donation of $40,000, a $30,000 bid for the East Florida Seminary land and the promise of free water for the university. The University of Florida officially opened on September 27, 1906 with 102 students.[10]

Gainesville changed greatly from 1900 to 1920. During that period, the infrastructure and support services were improved and modernized (e.g., disposal plant and sewerage system; fire engine) and new churches and a public library were built.[11] However, the county was hit with a terrible hurricane in 1926 that essentially ended the building boom that was taking place.[12] Consequently, Alachua County entered an economic depression three years before Wall Street crashed. [13]

However, the economic strain Florida was under during the Depression era was somewhat less visible in Gainesville and Alachua County due to the University of Florida. The University of Florida had a staff of 1000 and 3000 students that served as a source of revenue and kept Gainesville's economy from failing. In 1928, John Tigert became the University of Florida's president. He was instrumental in building a football stadium that seated 22,000 people, four student dorms, and an infirmary. The president also contributed to the creation of a student union. During his tenure, president Tigert transformed the university from a small college of 2,300 students to a major research institution of nearly 9,000 students.[14] The University emerged as the cultural center of the county and the state.[15] As Picard (1994) noted, Gainesville survived the 1930s and the Depression with minimal problems.[16]

Nevertheless, during World War II, the University of Florida student population dropped to approximately 1,600 students.[17] However, World War II also brought an influx of soldiers that served in the European and Pacific theaters, as Camp Blanding (the primary military reservation and training base for the Florida National Guard) is located approximately 30 miles from Gainesville.[18] In the years that followed the war, the University of Florida became an even more important factor in the county's economy. As a result of the GI Bill, many veterans came to the University of Florida to obtain a college degree. Between 1946 and 1947, the university's enrollment increased by 129 percent and army veterans represented more than half of the student body.[19] In 1947, co-ed enrollment was implemented at the university, additionally contributing to an increase in student population.[20]

Enlarged enrollment resulted in a post-war building boom in Alachua County. Outlying areas grew and in 1962 the city of Gainesville annexed 18 square miles of new housing developments. In 1965, the U.S Department of Education awarded a $400,000 grant to the University of Florida to establish the Graduate School and the Center for International Studies. As a result, by 1970, about 3,000 graduate students were taking classes at this university.[21] The significant growth experienced by the university directly and indirectly contributed to population increases and to the prosperity of Alachua County and Gainesville. In fact, by mid-1970s, a scholar who studied the economy of the area stated that "the University of Florida [was] without question the basic support and the main reason for the size and strength of the area."[22]

By 1970, 75 percent of the county's population resided in or around Gainesville city limits and the economy was dependent on the city's educational and medical facilities.[23] Expansion of educational and medical facilities in Alachua County contributed to increases in building construction and retail sales, and favored rising land values throughout the county. As a direct result of the construction of Shands, a teaching hospital at the University of Florida Medical Center, the US government decided to locate a new veterans' hospital in Gainesville.[24]

Modern Gainesville shows a shift in population and development. Western Gainesville started to develop around the Interstate-75 corridor. New housing developments such as the new urbanism developments of Haile Plantation and Town of Tioga were developed to the west of the city of Gainesville. In fact, both developments are not within the city limits of Gainesville but are considered in the county.

Just as many communities across the country have suffered through the current recession, Gainesville has also had its challenges. Although foreclosures in Florida are some of the highest in the country, Gainesville has not been impacted as much by the foreclosure crisis. One may surmise that the University of Florida, as a primary employer for the area, has prevented Gainesville from feeling the full brunt of the economic recession. Although new home development had slowed, developers in the Gainesville area are starting to purchase once dormant developments and are beginning to build new homes. According to the County Growth Management office, new home permits (74 permits) were up by 40 percent in the first three months of 2012, compared to the same period in 2011.[25] However, Gainesville could see major impacts of the recession in the near future as the state budget is formulated and there is discussion of extreme budget reductions to the University of Florida. The University of Florida is working hard to offset possible economic challenges to the area by creating economic and innovative incubators to launch high tech and bio-med businesses. Additionally, medical services also increase capacity as the US Veteran's Administration is near completion on a new bed tower to the Malcom Randall VA Medical Center. There is hope that the many educational, medical, and business assets in Gainesville will continue to support and allow the community to grow, thrive, and prosper.

University of Florida Community: Students, Faculty and Support Staff

Today, with approximately 50,000 students, the University of Florida is the fourth largest university in the United States. As of October 2010, the University of Florida had a total of 32,660 undergraduate students and 17,167 graduate and professional students. It is an NCAA Division 1 — A school making it part of the Southeastern Conference (SEC) with 18 collegiate campus sports — 8 men and 10 women (see www.ufl.edu). The University of Florida employs over 4,500 faculty and approximately 8,000 support staff. The University sits on about 2,000 acres and has more than 900 buildings, including 170 classrooms and laboratories. The National Register of Historic Places acknowledges the northeastern corner of the University's campus as a Historic District. Its residence halls house nearly 7,500 undergraduate students, while the campus' five family housing villages house about 1,000 married and/or graduate students.

Moving into the future, the University of Florida has initiated a project, the Innovation Square Incubator. This will be a 40-acre facility that focuses on research and high-tech companies. The building is located within walking distance of the university campus. The facility, which will have over 1 million square feet at completion will contain a business "super-incubator" to help launch high tech and bio-med businesses, funded using University of Florida research. It is projected that this public-private partnership between the University of Florida and private companies on site will create 3,000 new jobs in the area.[26]

Shands HealthCare and the University of Florida Health Science Center make up the University of Florida Academic Health Center. Shands HealthCare is one of the premiere health systems in the Southeast region of the United States. It is affiliated with the University of Florida Health Science Center. Shands HealthCare is actually comprised of nine not-for-profit hospitals located throughout the Southeast, and has a network of more than 80 primary and specialty practices and a medical staff of more than 1,500 affiliated University of Florida faculty and community physicians. Shands has a workforce of approximately 12,000 staff and serves over 85,000 admitted patients annually. The economic impact on communities by Shands HealthCare is notable. In 2010, Shands HealthCare programs had an economic impact of $1.9 billion and the organization spent $727 million in salaries and benefits to its workforce.[27]

Shands at the University of Florida is one of the private, not-for-profit hospitals that specialize in tertiary care for critically ill patients. It is one of the most comprehensive hospitals and one of the leading referral medical centers in the Southeast region. It is the primary teaching hospital for the University of Florida College of Medicine. Over 500 physicians work with healthcare professionals to provide quality care for patients. One of the newest additions has been the Shands Cancer Hospital at the University of Florida. Opened in November 2009, the hospital is located directly across the street from the Shands at the University of Florida medical center. This is a 500,000 square foot facility that houses 192 inpatient beds to meet the increased demand for cancer patient services.[28]

Seeds of New Urbanism in Gainesville

The best known new urbanism developments in Florida are Seaside, an unincorporated master-planned community in Walton County, which started to be developed in the early 1980s and Celebration (in Osceola County), a master-planned community that started to be built in 1996. Although several new residential subdivisions built in Gainesville during the construction boom of the late 1980s and early 1990s adopted features of new urbanism designs, two subdivisions — Haile Plantation, initially developed in the early 1990s and the Town of Tioga, initially developed in the late 1990s — adopted most of the new urbanism designs in their development pattern. Haile Plantation developed over the past two decades and currently includes about 3,000 homes, while the Town of Tioga started to be developed in 2000 on the outskirts of southwest Gainesville and includes about 300 homes.

Haile Plantation

The acreage that the new urbanist community, Haile Plantation, was developed on dates back to 1854, when Thomas Evans Haile established a 1500-acre Sea Island cotton plantation. After Thomas Haile died in the mid-1890s, the property was left to Evans Haile, the 14th of his fifteen children.[29] Nothing was done with the property, primarily a hardwood forest, until 1993 when Robert Kramer and Bob Rowe purchased 1,100 acres from the Haile family. Kramer and Rowe's desire was to build out a stable community at a rate of approximately 125 to 150 homes per year over 20 years. Currently, there are very few remaining lots available.

The primary objective of the developers was to build a community in which people could "work, shop, worship, attend school, enjoy outdoor recreation and leisure-time activities within a short walking distance or drive from their home." Another objective was to preserve, maintain and enhance the natural beauty of the land.[30]

Haile Plantation is located approximately five miles from the University of Florida and the city limits of Gainesville. It is within the urban growth boundary of Alachua County and is supported by services that were there prior to the start of the project.[31] Development in the direction of and past the Haile Plantation area has continued to grow as the growth of Alachua County moves westward.

Haile Plantation, itself, has many of the amenities one would find in a suburban development. There are a golf course, horse pastures, parks, walking trails and retail entities. The retail entities were originally established as part of the Haile Village Center. This is a 50 acre Village Center — approximately a half mile north to south. This is referred to as a five- minute neighborhood, as it is a five-minute walk from the center to the edge.[32]

Haile Village Center consists of single- and multi-family homes. It offers office, retail and civic uses within the village center. This is a mixed-use development, where office and retail spaces alternate with residential areas.[33] Kramer and Rowe used the example of St. Augustine, Florida and its development over 400 years in designing the Haile Community but on a much smaller scale. The community has a central square surrounded by civic buildings that host a police agency, the homeowners' association, and the community management.[34]

An important aspect of the design of Haile Village Center and the surrounding neighborhoods was to provide good transitions from the neighborhoods to the Village Center. A primary goal was to connect adjacent neighborhoods so residents could take care of their daily needs within a short walk of their home.[35] Currently, there are over 40 businesses in Haile Village Center that provide a multitude of services.

The design of the neighborhoods adjacent to the Haile Village Center follows the new urbanism tradition of the "live, work, and play" community concept. Housing prices range from $150,000 to more than $900,000; the homes are set close together with garages in rear alleyways and front porches are close to the street for "meeting and greeting" neighbors.[36] A street grid pattern is used to slow traffic and landscaping and parks are designed to create an aesthetically pleasing atmosphere.[37]

The Haile Plantation community consists of much more than just the Haile Village Center. There are over 50 very distinct neighborhoods surrounding Haile Village Center. Neighborhoods vary throughout the development. A neighborhood could be comprised of condominiums on the golf course and single houses of different types, while another is a gated community with a few million dollar homes. All neighborhoods are connected via sidewalks, trails or primary roads.

A recent addition to the development within the past few years was a market square located at the north end of the development. Not only are residents able to easily visit the locally owned shops and the weekly farmers' market in the Haile Village Center, but they now have access to a regional chain grocery store in the market square. One resident of Haile Plantation stated she often walks to the grocery store as it is only a 5-minute walk from her house. She often sees others walking, riding bicycles or golf carts to the market square. In addition to the regional chain grocery store, other retail and banking entities are available. The market square is located at a primary hub for the development as many Haile Plantation residents who work at the University of Florida or in the city of Gainesville transit this area on a daily basis.

Town of Tioga

The Town of Tioga was founded by Luis Diaz, the president of Gainesville's Dibros Corporation. The development's name actually comes from a former Florida city named Tioga that once existed not too far from the community that today shares its name. After selecting the city's name based on historical sources found at the Matheson Historical Center, Diaz worked with the U.S. Postal service to give the Town of Tioga its own zip code.[38]

The planning phase of Tioga began in 1994. When the idea of Tioga was first conceived, Diaz planned its construction over a 15-year period. During these 15 years, 537 homes along with a small retail center, health spa, and a school would be gradually built on 280 acres. The first phase anticipated the completion of 32 homes, while the second phase anticipated the completion of 40[39]. The first 32 homes would constitute the "Red Oak District." Diaz intended this district to be the most expensive in the planned community, with 1,800 to 3,700 square feet homes ranging in price from $150,000 to $375,000. When Diaz first began this endeavor, he both developed and supervised the construction of the homes alone. Soon, however, realizing the extent of his undertaking, Diaz solicited the help of Shelterwood Builders, Lyle Wilson Builder and Barry Rutenberg Homes.[40]

Tioga was planned to combine historical ambiance with small-town charm and "a touch of Frank Lloyd Wright prairie style;" "the cluster of houses on view may remind older generations of the homes they fondly remember from childhood, and new generations of the homes they long to cherish themselves."[41] Robert S. McCarter, University of Florida's College of Architecture chairman at the time the community started to be developed and a Frank Lloyd Wright expert actually designed one of the first built homes in Tioga. Using cultured stone and strong horizontal lines, McCarter wanted to emphasize naturalness.

Despite the nostalgic character of Tioga's first homes, the overall community does not exhibit one architectural style. One defining trait, however, is that most of Tioga's homes have two stories and porches in the front of the house and garages out back. Tioga homes are also deeper than they are wide. Diaz wanted to ensure that homes were not densely packed on small plots of land. As a result, there are only about two houses per acre making side yards visible from almost every room in a house. All houses also had to have a covered porch or a portico and a seven-by-seven deck leading to the front door to encourage neighbors to engage in conversation.[42]

The streets in Tioga are only about 20 feet wide with curbside green spaces adding an additional seven feet. Sidewalks are five feet wide allowing two individuals to walk side by side. Planners hoped that narrow streets and comfortable sidewalks would "discourage speed and unnecessary traffic" and would make Tioga a "pedestrian-friendly neighborhood."[43] As far as the mature oak trees that line some of the sidewalks, they were there before the builders started construction works. Diaz emphasized the importance of the location of such trees to ensure that builders "follow the natural lay of the land wherever possible."[44]

Tioga's grid-like street pattern, without any dead-ends or cul-de-sacs, also incorporates a network of alleys. Such alleys have eliminated a need for driveways, garages, and mailboxes to be placed at the front of a home.

In thinking about the future, Diaz wanted to ensure that no one street of the community could be deemed more important than another. Rather, he wanted to give Tioga residents choices. Diaz achieved this by building a two-mile long esplanade that sits at the foot of large oaks. This esplanade was designed to be within a five-minute radius of a Tioga Town Center and homes, so people could walk, jog, or bike everywhere they needed to go. In Tioga cars are not a necessity.

The main entrance to Tioga is directly across from West End Golf Course and passes through a commercial area. The lengthy entrance into Tioga is intended to act as a buffer to traffic noise. A fine detail of Tioga is its entrance sign that Diaz deliberately created to reflect "an all-new community" based on "old-fashioned values."[45]

Practices and Perceptions of New Urbanism in Gainesville, the University Town

The Developers: As stated previously, when Haile Plantation and Haile Village Center were presented, the developers Robert Kramer and Robert Rowe intended to create a community that would respect all the main principles of the new urbanism. One of the main goals of the developers was to create a "community to look as though it fit within the natural landscape and was not forced upon the land."[46] Green spaces, pedestrian friendly sidewalks, and the accommodation for future public transit were incorporated throughout these new planned communities. Robert Rowe noted that when developing Haile Plantation, one the most important objectives was to build a real community, not a simple neighborhood.

> Our goal was that it would develop a social fabric that would enrich
> the lives of its many residents. We wanted a variety of home prices,

sizes, and styles that would support a diverse population. We wanted a seamlessly integrated population to meet, greet, and know each other from meeting on the sidewalks and trails, at the Haile Village Center, the Haile Market Square and in using and being a part of the club amenities...Today, some thirty years from its beginning, I think by and large that our goals have been fulfilled...Haile Plantation remains uniquely special and, I think most will agree, pretty outstanding as evidenced by how well it has already stood the test of time.[47]

Luis Diaz, the mastermind behind the Town of Tioga, noted that when he started to develop Tioga there was "a lot of noise" regarding the new urbanism ideals. In order to avoid monotony, Diaz alternated different architectural styles and tried to build with flexibility. More importantly, he attempted to create an inclusive community, with "no segregation of values and economic statuses" among the town residents.[48]

Developing Tioga's homes with a "turn of the century for the next turn of the century" mindset, Diaz incorporated both "the new and the old." Prior to construction, everything on the lots that he and his builders were given was measured. In an interview with one of the authors, Diaz acknowledged that in the initial planning stages, he used as a source of inspiration R. G. Arendt's 1994 book *Rural by Design: Maintaining a Small Town Character.* Stimulated by Arendt who advocated creative, practical land-use planning techniques to preserve open space and community character, when planning Tioga Diaz tried to reinvent the design elements of the traditional town and adapt them to a modern community. In his view, houses had to reflect mixed values and different architectural styles and had to be "more welcoming than intimidating." For instance, garages were placed in the back of the house and front porches became a necessity to encourage conversations among neighbors. Diaz also conceived street corners with a tighter radius so cars would be forced to slowdown. Given Tioga's ample walking spaces, Diaz wanted to make sure people were safe when they used the sidewalks and crossed the streets. In addition, Diaz ensured that Tioga maintained a count of 20 percent of open space in its community, which has since become a law for builders in Alachua County.[49]

As far as the influence of University of Florida students and faculty go, Diaz sought their help as much as he could. In the planning stages, Diaz worked with Professor Orjan Wetterqvist, who was instrumental in the 1970s for stopping the division of the University campus into smaller units around Gainesville. Furthermore, student interns were used to conduct research and to obtain building permits for developments in Tioga. Although University of Florida faculty and students were not specifically targeted in Tioga's marketing campaigns, they did fall into the group of "college educated intellectuals," who were considered by developers some of Tioga's potential new residents. When interviewed, Diaz stated:

> We wanted people who would research and read consumer reports
> before making a home purchase. We wanted people who would be
> methodical in their purchase. We wanted someone who would be
> able to really appreciate the constructions based on the new urbanism
> ideas.[50]

Although they created two very different communities, the developers of
Haile Plantation and those who planned the Town of Tioga had very similar
visions and embraced similar ideals. Haile Plantation is several times the size of
the Town of Tioga resulting in hybrid new urbanism neighborhoods throughout
the development. However, one could view the Haile Village Center as being
quite similar to the Town of Tioga. Haile Village Center is small in scope, yet
has the same new urbanism amenities and features that Diaz has incorporated
into the Town of Tioga.

Residents who are University of Florida Employees: In order to learn which
factors were more likely to influence one's decision of buying a home in the
new urbanism communities of Haile Plantation and Town of Tioga, we
interviewed several residents who are employees of the University of Florida. In
most cases, the interviewed residents acknowledged that proximity to schools,
the amount of green space, the existence of walking paths, strict homeowner
covenants, and community amenities such as play grounds, tennis courts,
swimming pools were considered major attractions that made them purchase
houses in the new developments. All survey participants agreed that the
communities have incorporated new urbanism design features very well and that
the planners have done a great job in preserving the green spaces. One
respondent, a resident of Haile Plantation provided the following elaborate
comment:

> I believe Haile Village Center definitely meets all the criteria of the
> new urbanism model — tight walking neighborhoods, high density,
> front sidewalks, town square, etc. The surrounding neighborhoods are
> what I would consider a hybrid of new urbanism. For example, there
> are sidewalks that connect the many different neighborhoods but
> there aren't sidewalks within the neighborhoods. There are numerous
> parks and green space. In fact, one of the reasons we selected our
> home lot was the linear park that exists in front of it. The community
> amenities are convenient and easily accessible from the Haile
> neighborhoods. Oftentimes, you see individuals riding bikes, walking
> or using golf carts to go to the local grocery store (Publix—located at
> Haile Market Square) or down to the Haile Village Center for the
> weekly farmer's market or other retail outlets there. Although, the
> neighborhoods don't have sidewalks incorporated within them, my
> perception is that neighbors still meet and talk (often while taking
> walks or walking dogs). Funny anecdote: We have a cat that was an
> outdoor cat and everyone in the neighborhood knew Pierre (the cat).
> Pierre ran away and we started asking neighbors if they had seen him.
> Well, they hadn't, but they were happy to put up flyers, put out food

to entice him, or whatever. Anyway, eventually someone found him about 1.5 miles away and turned him into animal services where we bonded him out of jail. :) We have since turned Pierre into an indoor cat. Our neighbors continue to ask about him and how he is doing. This is the type of "neighborliness" that new urbanism encourages.

The large majority of respondents declared they were satisfied or very satisfied when they were asked to express their level of satisfaction with homeownership in a new urbanism community, with the design elements, the walking paths, the amount of green space, and the community amenities. One resident, however, responded that while she was highly satisfied with the walking paths in the community, she was dissatisfied that sidewalks lacked in her sub-division within the larger Haile Plantation community. We observed that while most of the earlier sub-divisions in Haile Plantation had elaborate sidewalks, the newer developments either have minimal sidewalk designs or no sidewalks at all. It appears that once the community was well established as a desirable residential area, later developments focused on maximizing the land space and profit and offered smaller lot sized homes with fewer or no sidewalks.

The new urbanism designs that appear to be preferred by most respondents are: walking paths/trails, multiple play grounds, green spaces with mature hardwood trees throughout the community, attempts to create private spaces between homes, the market square, and the existence of a country club. The majority of respondents declared that they will recommend their communities to potential home buyers, including their colleagues. In addition, the interviewees estimated that about half of the residents in their communities are University of Florida employees. Although subjective opinions, these answers suggests that University of Florida employees have played and may continue to play a vital role in the development and expansion of new urbanism communities in Gainesville.

The Realtors: In order to further verify the role of the University of Florida and its employees in new urbanism development of Gainesville, we interviewed two realtors with a combined experience of 27 years serving home buyers in Gainesville and Alachua County. In their average estimate, about one fourth of Gainesville's residential real estate market is currently occupied by University of Florida employees. They concur that Haile Plantation and the Town of Tioga have incorporated the new urbanism features of public/open spaces, mixed use patterns, walkable neighborhoods, and context appropriate architecture.

To a question of whether these new urbanism communities are among the most definite residential areas that they would show to prospective home buyers who are University of Florida employees, interestingly, both realtors responded 'no.' The realtors explained that they deal with a variety of University of Florida employees, who have different income levels and that not all of them could afford homes in these new urbanism communities. In addition, the realtors noted that new urbanism does not appeal to all home buyers. Nonetheless, both realtors agreed that the new urbanism features of Haile Plantation and the Town of Tioga attract a relatively large proportion of University of Florida employees in search of a new house. According to their estimates, about 35 percent of Haile Plantation residents and about 25 percent of the Town of Tioga residents are University of Florida employees. However, both respondents acknowledged that during the past five years less than 25 percent of their new clients who were University of Florida employees actually bought homes in these new urbanism communities. Finally, both interviewees concurred that the new developments within Haile Plantation have lesser new urbanism features than the older developments.

Conclusion

During the past three decades, new urbanism concepts, features, and design elements have been adopted into various residential developments at various degrees. While it has attracted developers and a niche group of home buyers, new urbanism has also attracted criticisms for being 'too much involved in planning.' Due to land use for community spaces such as walking paths, green spaces, play grounds and other amenities, developing new urbanism communities is based on land availability or conversion, making it a more expensive process than standard residential developments. As a result, only developers who truly believe that new urbanism ideas are valid would engage in an endeavor whose final results remain unpredictable, especially during periods of economic scarcity. Most 'high volume' developers tend to shy away from developments with large land areas dedicated to community space. The higher price tag of developing new urbanism communities eventually trickles down to the home buyers who can afford them. It appears that new urbanism developments are not for everyone and not even for all the families who can afford homes in the newly planned communities. It takes a distinctive mindset, a specific taste and a certain lifestyle for individuals and families to be attracted to new urbanism communities. In order to create thriving new urbanism communities, developers also need conducive land use policies and local political support.

The university town of Gainesville has developers who believe in new urbanism and are willing to invest in residential developments that incorporate its design elements. Political leadership and planning experts in Gainesville fully support the idea of housing developments with new urbanism features. Developers are required to preserve a certain amount of green space within their development, neighborhoods must be connected, home lot sizes are smaller and transportation nodes must be considered. However, that being said, there is also a culture within Gainesville and the university community where individuals prefer to live in large spread-out developments with large lots so one can experience his/her own green space without having to share it with other residents.

Small and medium size university towns have sufficient land available for new developments in their immediate surroundings and/or within their suburban reach. While empirical studies have not been conducted on university employees' preferences for new urbanism communities, there is a belief that university faculty and professionals may gravitate toward this type of communities. The cases of Haile Plantation and the Town of Tioga presented in this chapter appear to support this assumption. Even in new urbanism communities, later developments or expansions of residential units may or may not incorporate the original design elements due to land availability and market demands. Haile Plantation, which has been developed over the past 20 years, is an example of this. Our data indicate that, compared to early developments, more recent residential sub-divisions developed by individual builders have lesser amenities, such as sidewalks and have smaller lot sizes. However, the original community amenities such as walking trails, shopping areas, play grounds, etc. are still available to residents and continue to attract home buyers. In contrast to Haile Plantation, the Town of Tioga continues to develop based on the original new urbanism concepts (e.g., walkable neighborhoods, front porches, green spaces, and retail areas). The homes being built currently still meet the design criteria established by the developer more than a decade ago. It remains unclear and further research is needed to determine why new developments in the Town of Tioga continue to follow the original concept, while in Haile Plantation the original planning and designs suffered alterations.

The future of additional new urbanism developments in the university town of Gainesville is questionable. Although Haile Plantation and Town of Tioga continue to develop, due to the impacts of economic recession and home mortgage crisis there are as many houses in those developments that are for sale, in short sale, or in foreclosure as one might find in other residential communities across the country. When driving around the area, in many places where numerous new housing developments were started not long ago, one can easily notice that no construction is taking place. Additionally, the retail areas have experienced challenges. Residents have seen businesses come and go in the retail areas of Haile and Tioga as businesses struggle to survive in these times of economic hardship.

Furthermore, severe budget cuts will soon affect all public universities in Florida, University of Florida included. Consequently, university employees who could afford to purchase homes in a new urbanism community might be apprehensive about purchasing any home at this point in time. Although we believe that new urbanism developments in university towns are considered desirable by a large number of university employees, who have the potential to make the neo-traditional developments economically viable, we also anticipate that until the economy turns around, current new urbanism communities are less likely to grow and additional new urbanism communities are less likely to be built.

Notes

1. Hampton, G. and Hingham, D. (1999). The Impact of an Urban University on Community Development. Retrieved fromhttp://www.umdnj.edu/comreweb/pdf/The_Impact_of_an_Urban%20University.PDF.

2. Hampton and Hingham, *op.cit.*

3. Hampton and Hingham, *op. cit.*

4. Wiewel, W. and Knaap, G. *Partnership for Smart Growth: University-Community Collaboration for Better Public Places,* (Armonk, NY: M.E. Sharpe, 2005).

5. Perry, D. and Wiewel, W. *The University as Urban Developer: Case Studies and Analysis,* (Armonk, NY: M.E.Sharpe, 2005).

6. Sperling, B. and Sander, P. *Cities Ranked & Rated* (second edition). (Hoboken, NJ: Wiley Publishing, Inc., 2007).

7. LaCoe, N. (1974). The Alachua frontier. In J. B. Opdyke (Ed.), *Alachua County: A Sesquicentennial Tribute.* Gainesville, FL: The Alachua County Historical Commission.

8. Picard, John B. *Florida's Eden — An Illustrated History of Alachua County,* (Gainesville, FL: Maupin House, 1994); Ellerbe, H.C. (1974). Statehood, Secession and Reconstruction. In J. B. Opdyke (Ed.), *Alachua County: A Sesquicentennial Tribute.* Gainesville, FL: The Alachua County Historical Commission.

9. Picard, *op.cit.*

10. Picard, *op.cit.*

11. Picard, *op.cit.*

12. Drylie, S. (1974). Alachua County, 1880-1900. In J. B. Opdyke (Ed.), *Alachua County: A Sesquicentennial Tribute.* Gainesville, FL: The Alachua County Historical Commission.

13. Picard, *op. cit.*

14. Picard, *op. cit.*

15. Drylie, *op. cit.*

16. Picard, *op. cit.*

17. Picard, *op. cit.*

18. Drylie, *op. cit.*

19. Spencer, A.P. (1974). The World Wars. In J. B. Opdyke (Ed.), *Alachua County: A Sesquicentennial Tribute.*Gainesville, FL: The Alachua County Historical Commission.

20. Picard, *op. cit.*

21. *Alligator* (April 11, 2011). "This Week in Gainesville..." University of Florida Students News Paper.

22. Cox, M.G. (1974). Economic, political and social developments since World War II. In J. B. Opdyke (Ed.), *Alachua County: A Sesquicentennial Tribute.* Gainesville, FL: The Alachua County Historical Commission, pp. 47.

23. Picard, *op. cit.*

24. Cox, *op. cit.*

25. Clark, A. (2012, April 29). Some welcome signs of life in new home markets. *Gainesville Sun.* Retrieved from http://www.gainesville.com/article/20120429/ARTICLES/120429551.

26. Innovation Square (2010). *Site Plan.* Retrieved from http://www.innovationsquare.ufl.edu.

27. Shands HealthCare (2010). *Shands HealthCare and the University of Florida health Science Center 2010 Community Benefit Report.* Retrieved from http://www.shands.org/about/community benefit/2010/default.asp.

28. Shands HealthCare, *op. cit.*
29. Haile Homestead: http://www.hailehomestead.org.
30. Kramer, R. *Breaking the Habit of Suburbia.* Atlanta, Georgia. February 11, 2001. Presentation. Retrieved from http://www.webenet.com/newurbanism.htm.
31. Kramer, *op. cit.*
32. Kramer, *op. cit.*
33. Kramer, *op. cit.*
34. Kramer, *op.cit.*
35. Kramer, *op. cit.*
36. Deere, as quoted in Harris, M. (2007, August 9). Haile Village Center brings residents and businesses together with New Urbanism concept. *The Gainesville Sun.* Retrieved from http://www.gainesville.com/article/20070809/NEWS/708090305?Title=Haile-Village-Center-brings-residents-and-businesses-together-with-New-Urbanism-concept.
37. Harris, *op. cit.*
38. Morgan, N. (1997, March 9). A sense of place. *The Gainesville Sun.* Retrieved from http://www.gainesville.com/section/search04?q=town%20of%20tioga.
39. Morgan, *op.cit.*
40. Morgan, *op. cit.*
41. Morgan, *op. cit.*
42. Morgan, *op. cit.*
43. Morgan, *op. cit.*
44. Morgan, *op. cit.*
45. Morgan, *op. cit.*
46. Rowe, Robert (2010, November 21). [Letter to Wes White]. Retrieved from http://www.hailewest.org.
47. Rowe, *op. cit.*
48. Luis Diaz, interviewed by Kimberly Ambayec, 2011.
49. Luis Diaz, interviewed by Kimberly Ambayec, 2011.
50. Luis Diaz, interviewed by Kimberly Ambayec, 2011.

Chapter Eight

Building Community: Residential Satisfaction in Conventional and Neotraditional Suburban Neighborhoods

John Vick and Douglas Perkins

Introduction

In recent decades the *New Urbanism* movement has fueled new forms of neighborhood design and development whose guiding principles include providing more and better local amenities and walkability, and increasing resident social interaction and sense of community, thereby improving the overall quality of life in communities.[1] These neighborhoods are often referred to as Traditional Neighborhood Developments (TND), Neotraditional Developments (NTD), or simply new urban neighborhoods. This type of development runs contrary to the primary building type of the latter half of the 20th century, the suburban neighborhood type.

Neighborhood Types

The term *urban* can be defined in various ways. We use it to refer to the layout of the built environment, which is determined by factors such as density, pedestrian orientation, and land use. Characteristics of the urban environment include: medium to high-density buildings; sidewalks; mixed-use on the building, block, or neighborhood level; a pedestrian orientation; front porches and short set-backs from the street; connected street networks; and open public spaces.

In contrast to the urban neighborhood type, the suburban model is a relatively recent form of development. It emerged after World War II in response to pent up housing demand, the baby boom, a booming growth-based consumer economy, and government lending and tax policies. Land outside the urban core was cheaper and available in large tracts. Automobiles began to replace public transit and walking as the primary mode of transportation. The suburban model is uniquely car-oriented, regulating the built environment both in scale and functionality to give priority to drivers. Suburban environments are defined by low building density (single-family detached homes); buildings set back from the street with parking or large lawns in front; segregated uses (retail, office, and residential split up into distinct areas); and few or no sidewalks. Residential streetscapes became more dominated by attached garages than front porches. New urbanists criticize the suburban model as hindering social interaction, leading to a diminished sense of community.

Research on Environmental Design and Sense of Community

Sense of community has been extensively researched and linked to numerous social and neighborhood conditions including the physical environment, mainly focusing on pedestrian orientation (neighborhood character, architectural design and quality, availability of public space, local stores and amenities), the social environment (social interaction, neighboring, neighborhood cohesion, community organizing, community identity, residential satisfaction), and individual factors (well-being, physical and mental health, attitudes toward neighbors, attraction to neighborhood, community identity, and place attachment).[2] Perhaps the most important of those conditions for sense of community is social interaction.[3] A central question and longstanding debate is whether, or how much, environmental planning and design can influence the frequency and/or quality of social interaction and, through it, sense of community.

Although strengthening sense of community has been widely used as a justification by planners and developers for building neighborhoods with urban characteristics, what is the evidence supporting such a link? Some studies have compared urban and suburban neighborhood types while others have evaluated specific characteristics of those types, such as pedestrian orientation, density, public meeting spaces, and street layout.

Studies of New Urban Communities

Plas and Lewis (1996) interviewed residents of Seaside, Florida, a New Urban neighborhood specifically designed to promote sense of community.[4] The neighborhood design elements include traditional architecture and materials, large front porches, homes built up to sidewalks, a low picket fence around every front yard, a mix of uses (residential, commercial, retail, open community space), a hexagonal street grid, and streets that are hospitable for pedestrians and inhospitable for automobiles, among others. While it was originally intended to be a mixed-income neighborhood, Seaside has become an upscale community that consists primarily of vacation homes. It has 10 neighborhood associations and residents are highly active in the community. The study found that physical characteristics of the neighborhood appeared to play a role in the development of sense of community. When asked about their experience of living in the neighborhood, participants in the study noted feelings of neighborliness, togetherness, community sharing, and loyalty.

Studies have also been conducted that compare new urban and suburban neighborhoods on sense of community and other social constructs. Brown and Cropper (2001) evaluated sense of community and neighboring behavior by comparing a neotraditional subdivision with a conventional suburban subdivision. Although both neighborhoods had sidewalks, the new urban subdivision had numerous pedestrian-oriented features and a higher density that the suburban subdivision lacked. No difference was found between the neighborhoods on sense of community, but the new urban subdivision had significantly higher neighboring behavior and outdoor use.[5] Similarly, Kim and Kaplan (2004) compared a new urbanist community with a suburban development on sense of community. The neighborhoods differed in terms of density, lot sizes, variety of land uses, and open space. The survey questions assessed the role of physical characteristics related to site development, site design, circulation, amenities, and architectural design. Respondents were asked about the importance of each of these characteristics. Results showed a substantially higher sense of community in the new urban community, a finding that was corroborated by in-person interviews with residents. However, of the dimensions of sense of community, social interaction did not appear to play a strong role in improving sense of community, even though interactions with next-door neighbors did play a strong role.[6] One of the primary concerns with these comparison studies is that of *self-selection*. Critics argue that residents who live in new urban neighborhoods will participate in behaviors associated with those types of neighborhoods because they are seeking out a neighborhood that facilitates that lifestyle. Conversely, residents of typical suburban neighborhoods would not choose that lifestyle. Thus, residents are essentially self-selecting themselves into their respective neighborhoods and any inter-community differences may be caused by the residents' neighborhood selection and not by the physical characteristics of those neighborhoods.

Mixed-Use Development

Nasar and Julian (1995) conducted two studies examining sense of community. The first evaluated residents in neighborhoods with varying levels of mixed-use development to assess differences in sense of community. The term *mixed-use* refers to developments that combine multiple uses such as residential, commercial, or retail. Results showed significantly less sense of community in the single-use areas when compared to those areas with three or four uses. A second study found that residents of an apartment building containing an outdoor courtyard felt a significantly higher sense of community than comparable residents in an interior corridor building.[7] The findings suggest that the presence of an open, outdoor public meeting space, a key feature of urban environments, may lead to higher levels of sense of community.

Density and Pedestrian Orientation

Density is one of the key features that distinguish urban from suburban environments. Freeman (2001) compared four major metropolitan areas on social ties in neighborhoods of varying density. The results showed that residential density was not strongly related to the formation of social ties.

However, the relationship with whether or not a resident had to drive to and from work was important. Freeman concludes that developing more transit-oriented neighborhoods, characteristic of urban environments, would likely increase social ties.[8]

Another integral feature of urban neighborhoods is a pedestrian-oriented environment. Lund (2002) compared a pedestrian-oriented neighborhood of urban design with a suburban automobile-oriented neighborhood and found a significantly higher sense of community in the pedestrian-oriented neighborhood compared to the automobile-oriented neighborhood.[9]

Outdoor and Public Space

Another common feature of urban environments is usable open space, or parks, plazas, and playgrounds. Skjaeveland(2001) examined street parks to evaluate social interactions among neighbors, a pedestrian-friendly element that is characteristic of urban environments. The study looked at sections of three residential streets that were converted into street parks that involved considerable changes in spatial layout, and were compared to two control groups. Overall, increased neighborhood involvement was observed at the street park sites, but increased social ties only increased for some people. The author suggests that the symbolic change may be more significant than the functional effects, and could play a key role in formation of neighborhood identity.[10] Kuo *et al.* (1998) also examined the use of common or meeting spaces with a particular focus on the levels of vegetation present in the space. The results indicated that more vegetation was associated with more use of common space, which led to more socialization and a greater sense of community.[11]

Research Literature: Summary and Conclusions

The literature comparing the effects of urban and suburban neighborhood characteristics on sense of community shows mixed results, but reveals some insights. Table 8.1 presents a summary of the findings for the studies reviewed here that examined the sense of community in different types of neighborhoods.

When comparing urban and suburban environments, several studies found a significantly higher sense of community in those areas with new urbanist characteristics.[12] Some studies also found that social ties[13] and neighborhood involvement[14] are higher in urban compared to suburban environments. Brown and Cropper (2001) found no difference in sense of community between a new urbanist and a traditional suburban development, but did find more neighboring behavior in the former suggesting either that sense of community takes more time to develop or that one does not always lead to the other.[15]

Overall, these studies point to a relationship between characteristics of the built environment and sense of community. The specific nature of this relationship, however, is still unclear. In general, it appears that there may be some merit to the new urbanists' claim that urban neighborhoods foster a stronger sense of community than typical suburban neighborhoods, but more research is needed to support and clarify this assertion.

Table 8.1: Effects of Neighborhood Design on Sense of Community

Study	Study focus	Results
Plas and Lewis (1996)	New urban town	Neighborhood characteristics appeared to promote development of sense of community
Brown and Cropper (2001)	New urban subdivision vs. suburban subdivision	No difference in sense of community. Higher neighboring and outdoor use in New Urban neighborhood
Kim and Kaplan (2004)	New urban subdivision vs. suburban subdivision	Significantly higher sense of community in the urban neighborhood
Nasar and Julian (1995) Study 1	Neighborhoods with varying levels of mixed-use development	Significantly higher sense of community in mixed-use neighborhoods
Nasar and Julian (1995) Study 2	Buildings with outdoor courtyard vs. interior hallway	Significantly higher sense of community in a building with an outdoor courtyard
Lund (2002)	Pedestrian-oriented neighborhood vs. automobile-oriented neighborhood	Significantly higher sense of community in pedestrian-oriented neighborhood
Kuo et al. (1998)	Levels of vegetation around buildings	More vegetation linked to more social interaction leading to increase in sense of community
Freeman (2001)	Neighborhoods with varying density	Residential density not significant in the formation of social ties. More social ties for those who do not have to drive to work
Skjaeveland (2001)	Neighborhoods with street parks (public spaces) vs. no street parks	Significant increase in neighborhood involvement in neighborhoods with street parks

Purpose of the Study

The study builds on literature suggesting that neighborhood design, including the layout, physical characteristics, and amenities of a neighborhood, can significantly influence resident perceptions, attitudes and subjective qualities of community life. The purpose of the study is to determine whether residents in a new urbanist-designed neighborhood experience more home and community satisfaction, sense of community and neighboring than do residents in a demographically comparable suburban development.

In order to better understand the mechanism for any differences we find in such qualities, we will also look for differences between the communities in how often residents visit with neighbors, walk in their neighborhood, look after a neighbor's house, participate in neighborhood or group activities, and how they feel about various aspects of their neighborhood's design and function. This study was developed with, and funded by, a developer that currently builds both new urban and typical suburban planned communities.

Methods

Site Selection

In order to determine the effects of neighborhood design on social quality of life, we selected two neighborhoods that differ in terms of neighborhood design. The first neighborhood, New Urbana (pseudonym), is a Traditional Neighborhood Development (TND), which was designed following the principles of new urbanism. The second neighborhood is Southwood Estates (pseudonym), a neighborhood built according to typical suburban design principles. The neighborhoods were chosen to be similar in terms of location (county), income, race, size and quality of homes, and geographic size. Both are in the metropolitan area of the same medium-sized, mid-South U.S. city, and are approximately the same distance from the urban core. The most notable difference between the neighborhoods, other than the design, is the population density and the number of homes. At the time of the study New Urbana had approximately 735 homes, while SouthwoodEstates had approximately 190. In addition, Southwood Estates is older, constructed primarily in the late 1980's and 1990's, while New Urbana was still under construction (although mostly complete) at the time of the survey.

Participants

We recruited residents from each neighborhood primarily through email and phone, although a few were recruited in person at their homes. A total of 170 (out of 735) New Urbana households and 140 (out of 190) Southwood Estates households were selected at random and contacted to participate in the study. We conducted 26 long-form surveys (15 in New Urbana; 11 in Southwood

Estates) and an additional 38 short-form surveys from New Urbana households. Although the sample is relatively small (N =64), it offers an adequate representation of the areas under study.

Neighborhood Similarities and Differences

There were no statistically significant differences between neighborhoods on income, race, gender, age, years of education, number of children, homeownership, whether or not a close family member lives in the neighborhood, or household size. All survey respondents were white and owned their homes. There was a statistically significant difference between the neighborhoods regarding the respondents' length of residence. Southwood Estates residents have lived in their neighborhood an average of approximately 12 years, while New Urbana residents have lived in their neighborhood about two and a half years, on average. All else equal, an increase in the average tenure in the suburban neighborhood was associated with a positive view of the neighborhood on all study variables; thus, if the New Urban neighborhood would have even the same average level of residential satisfaction, sense of community, or neighboring, that would be noteworthy.

Survey Measures

The survey was developed by the researchers in partnership with the local developer who funded the study. The short version of the survey used for the present study includes questions on home and neighborhood satisfaction, neighborhood preferences, neighborhood qualities/amenities, sense of community, walking and neighboring behavior, social interaction, demographics, and other items not used here (the indicators are presented in Table 8.2). Most survey questions are multiple choice, but open-ended questions were also included so that residents could describe their neighborhood experiences and perceptions.

Results

Sense of Community

Neighborhood mean comparisons appear in Table 8.2. New Urbana residents indicated significantly more often than Southwood Estates residents that people in their neighborhood generally watch after each other and help out when they can, and that they feel a strong sense of community with others in their neighborhood.

Home and Neighborhood Satisfaction

Residents were asked to rate their satisfaction with: their house as a place to live; their neighborhood as a place to live; and their neighborhood as a place to raise children. New Urbana residents rated their homes and neighborhoods marginally higher than did Southwood Estates residents, although differences were not statistically significant due in part to the very high level of satisfaction in both neighborhoods (average ratings over 9 out of 10).

Neighborhood Qualities and Amenities

Residents were asked to indicate what amenities can be found in their neighborhood and had to also rate the quality of the amenities (e.g., nearby parks and playgrounds, availability of needed stores, and activities for youth after school) existent in their neighborhood. Results showed that New Urbana residents had significantly more parks and playgrounds in their neighborhood than residents from the comparison neighborhood. Additionally, the quality of these amenities was superior in New Urbana.

Neighborhood Preferences

Residents in both neighborhoods were asked if they preferred to live in a dense, mixed-use neighborhood rather than in a low-density neighborhood with separated uses. Preference for mixed-use developments was significantly higher among New Urbana residents when compared to Southwood Estates residents.

Walking

Respondents were asked how often they walk in their neighborhood. Results indicate that New Urbana residents walk significantly more often than Southwood Estates residents.

Neighboring Behavior

Residents were asked how many times in the past year they had borrowed something from (or loaned something to) a neighbor, visited with neighbors, had spoken with a neighbor about a problem, and kept watch on a neighbor's house while the neighbors were away. While New Urbana residents did visit with their neighbors significantly more often than residents in Southwood Estates, there were no significant inter-group differences regarding the other measures of neighboring behavior.

Table 8.2: Neighborhood Comparisons on Key Variables

Question (possible range)	New Urbana (n=51)	Southwood Estates (n=11)	
	Mean (SD)	Mean (SD)	p
How satisfied are you with your house as a place to live? (1-10)	9.16 (1.08)	9.09 (1.04)	ns
How satisfied are you with your neighborhood as a place to live? (1-10)	9.36 (1.03)	9.18 (1.08)	ns
How satisfied are you with your neighborhood as a place to raise children? (1-10)	9.36 (1.13)	9.18 (1.08)	ns
I feel a strong sense of community with others in my neighborhood (1-5)	4.41 (.85)	3.45(1.04)	.002**
People in my neighborhood watch after each other and help out when they can. (1-5)	4.63 (.94)	3.91 (.54)	.02*
It is important to me to feel a sense of community with the people in my neighborhood.	4.67 (.49)	3.55 (1.04)	.001***
How often do you walk in your neighborhood? (1=never to 5=every day)	4.37 (.87)	3.73 (.90)	.03*⁺
How many times in the past 12 months did you borrow something from or loan something to a neighbor?	2.67 (1.01)	2.18 (.75)	ns
How many times in the past 12 months did you visit with neighbors?	4.28 (.90)	3.45 (1.04)	.01**
How many times in the past 12 months did you speak with a neighbor about a neighborhood problem?	2.85 (1.05)	2.73 (1.10)	ns
How many times in the past 12 months did you keep watch on a neighbor's home while they're away?	2.65 (.93)	2.73 (1.19)	ns
I prefer dense, mixed-use neighborhoods to neighborhoods where commercial, office, and residential uses are apart from one another. (1-5)	4.31 (1.18)	3.00 (.89)	.001***
How would you rate the availability of neaby parks and playgrounds in your neighborhood? (1-10)	9.28 (.90)	8.45 (2.02)	.04*
How would you rate the housing quality in your neighborhood? (1-10)	9.00 (1.18)	8.70 (.95)	ns

* p≤.05, **p≤.01, ***p≤.001 (2-tail test)
⁺difference not significant when excluding those reporting sense of community or new urbanist features as a reason for moving to the current neighborhood.

Neighborhood Involvement

Questions included only in the long form of the survey were less likely to show significant inter-group differences due to the smaller samples, but the questions focusing on neighborhood involvement did reveal significant differences. When asked if they participate in more activities than they did in their previous neighborhood, New Urbana residents were significantly more likely to answer 'yes' than their counterparts in Southwood Estates. There was also a significant difference between neighborhoods on whether or not residents participate in neighborhood meetings or activities in their neighborhood. However, no significant inter-group differences were obtained when neighborhoods were compared in terms of residents' membership in neighborhood groups or organizations.

Residents in both neighborhoods were asked to write down the types of neighborhood activities they are involved in (responses are listed in Table 8.3). Overall, Southwood Estates residents appear more likely to participate in organizational meetings, whereas New Urbana residents appear to be more active in recreational clubs, events, and classes. In general, New Urbana residents participate in neighborhood activities more frequently (weekly or multiple times a week), whereas Southwood Estates residents most often participate in monthly or annual events.

Table 8.3: Activities Registered in Each Neighborhood

New Urbana		Southwood Estates
Exercise Class	Dancing	Women's Association
HOA Meetings	Town Hall Meetings	Bunko
Bible Study	Gardening Class	HOA Board and Meetings
Potlucks	Book Club	Petitioning
Voting	MahJongg	Holiday Parties
Financial Committee	Bunko	Children's Parties
Welcome Committee	Wine Club	Lunches
Block Parties	Holiday Home Tour	Informal Parties
Holiday Parties	Informal Parties	
Pool/Swimming	Green Committee	
Movies	Golf Club	
Concerts	Motorcycle Club	
Scrapbooking	Courtyard Garden Tour	
St. Jude's	Pumpkin Path	

Experiential Account of Life in the Neighborhood

Residents of both neighborhoods were asked to write about their family's experience of living in their neighborhood. They also had an opportunity to write any additional comments about their neighborhood at the end of the survey. New Urbana residents overwhelmingly expressed positive feelings about their neighborhood, particularly amenities, closeness with neighbors, activities and events, safety, child-friendliness, and walkability. Although there are numerous mentions of architecture, landscaping, and other physical features, most comments are about the social and community life of the neighborhood; visiting with neighbors, participating in classes and activities, looking out for one another, etc. A New Urbana resident gave the following response when asked about his experience of living in the neighborhood:

> We all enjoy living here. I met more neighbors in the first few months here than I met in 3 years at the previous house. We take tennis lessons, use the clubhouse (fitness room and classes), attend events at the clubhouse, and use the pools regularly. We especially like the social interaction in the alley behind our house (the neighbors hang out, chat, and watch the kids). When we walk, we stop and talk to people in their yards and on their porches. We also have a lot of fun on Halloween and other holidays due to the foot traffic in the neighborhood. None of us have any real complaints. All of us like this neighborhood better than anywhere else we've lived. (New Urbana resident interview)[16]

There were a few criticisms as well. Residents noted problems with landscaping being maintained, neighbors who complain too much, and the neighborhood becoming too large. For instance, a long-term resident noted a diminished sense of community and closeness with neighbors as the neighborhood has grown in size. Several residents acknowledged the lack of racial, religious, and economic diversity as a problem in their neighborhood and pointed out that an increasing number of the newer homes mostly attract affluent residents. Many residents specifically mentioned that they chose to live in New Urbana because it was built based on a traditional neighborhood design (TND). However, some residents declared that the neighborhood has strayed from its original design and intent, to its detriment.

Southwood Estates residents also responded positively to the questions regarding one's life experiences in the neighborhood. Yet, these responses were much shorter and less detailed than those given by the New Urbana residents. Many of the residents of the conventional suburban neighborhood noted that Southwood Estates is a great neighborhood. Although some respondents said they were thankful to live in this particular neighborhood, others wished there were more amenities, such as a pool or a clubhouse. To reiterate, the most striking inter-group difference refers to the quality of the answers volunteered by the residents of the comparison sites. While New Urbana respondents often included stories to better illustrate their contentment with the neighborhood, the interviwees from Southwood Estates tended to formulate only succinct statements to indicate their residential satisfaction.

Reasons for Moving to Neighborhood

Residents were also asked what motivated them to move to their neighborhood. New Urbana residents noted an array of motivating factors, including landscaping, neighborhood amenities, architecture, sense of community, walkability, investment, kid-friendliness, and neighborhood activities, among others. On the other hand, access to the interstate, large lots, and the size of homes were the main factors that influenced the relocation decisions of Southwood Estates residents.

Self-Selection

One of the problems with comparing two different types of neighborhoods on sense of community is that residents who want to live in a neighborhood characterized by a strong sense of community or those who wish to be involved in neighborhood activities, will move to a neighborhood that is specifically designed to promote or enhance those things. In other words, it is possible that a process of *self-selection* takes place with respect to individuals who decide to live in a neotraditional community. Residents of the new urbanist communities may perceive their neighbors as being more involved in the neighborhood activities and may appreciate a stronger sense of community because they were interested to live in places characterized by frequent social interaction in the first place.

Most studies that have compared new urbanist suburban neighborhoods to typical suburban neighborhoods have not accounted for this issue. In order to control for the influence of self-selection, we asked residents what motivated them to move to their present neighborhood. Those New Urbana residents who said they moved there specifically seeking a sense of community were excluded in a second analysis of the data. Residents who specifically noted that New Urbana was built in accordance with a traditional neighborhood design (TND) were also excluded, since use of that terminology implies respondents were familiar with the intent of the neighborhood design, which is to promote a sense of community.

In the original analysis, New Urbana residents reported walking significantly more often than Southwood Estates residents. When respondents familiar with new urbanist principles and those looking for more intense social interaction were excluded from the analysis, results showed no difference regarding the residents' frequency of walking when the neighborhoods were compared. This seems to indicate that those New Urbana residents who walked the most in the neighborhood were those who specifically sought out a neighborhood like New Urbana that intends to promote a sense of community. The findings from the analysis that excluded respondents considered self-selected residents are perhaps most relevant. Specifically, even when accounting for those residents who purposely moved to New Urbana for a sense of community there were still several significant differences between neighborhoods. This seems to indicate that neighborhood design does play a role in residents' social behavior and quality of life.

Discussion

The purpose of the study was to determine whether or not neighborhood design influences social indicators of community life, specifically neighborhood satisfaction, neighborhood amenities, neighborhood preference, walking, neighboring behavior, and neighborhood involvement. With regards to sense of community, some key statistically significant differences exist between the neighborhoods. Compared to Southwood Estates, New Urbana residents were significantly more likely to generally watch after each other and help out when they could. Residents of the new urbanist community also perceived a stronger sense of community in their neighborhood and visited with their neighbors significantly more often than Southwood Estates residents. While New Urbana residents rated neighborhood satisfaction higher than those in Southwood Estates the difference was not statistically significant.

Taken together, these findings seem to indicate that New Urbana residents do in fact feel a stronger sense of community with others in their neighborhood than residents of Southwood Estates. These findings are also supported by the residents' accounts of their experiences with neighborhood living. While Southwood Estates residents seem happy with their neighborhood and have few negative things to say about their experience of living there, New Urbana residents describe their experiences in detail and often with overwhelming pride and affection. However, some New Urbana residents were also critical of the neighborhood; specifically, these residents mentioned the lack of socio-economic diversity and changes in sense of community and neighboring behavior as the neighborhood has grown. Several residents noted the lack of religious, ethnic, and income diversity as a problem for the neighborhood, a problem that has unfortunately been observed in new urbanist developments nationwide.[17] Another long-time resident also noted that, as the neighborhood has grown in size, the sense of community has diminished. These may be important points to consider when planning future New Urban developments. It is also important to note that a number of residents from both neighborhoods asked to view the results of this study, which indicates interest in the study topic from both New Urbana and Southwood Estates residents. While collecting data for the study, we also received responses from residents of both neighborhoods who offered help in contacting other residents or providing other useful information for the study.

New Urbana residents appear to be significantly more involved in neighborhood activities than Southwood Estates residents. Additionaly, the residents of the New Urbana are involved in more community activities than they were in their previous neighborhood. New Urbana residents also participate in neighborhood activities more frequently than Southwood Estates residents, although this seems to be primarily due to the types of activities available in each neighborhood. New Urbana activities include more classes, recreation, and use of neighborhood amenities. Southwood Estates residents are active in their HOA and other neighborhood meetings, but they do not have amenities (pool, clubhouse, etc) for recreation and other socializing. Southwood Estates residents noted the lack of amenities as a negative aspect of their neighborhood when describing their experience of living there.

Regarding neighborhood preferences, New Urbana residents were significantly more likely than their Southwood Estates counterparts to prefer living in a dense, mixed-use neighborhood. This is perhaps not surprising since residents who live in a neighborhood with these characteristics chose to live in a new urbanist community and not in a more typical suburban neighborhood. Most New Urbana residents also visit the neighborhood businesses, and those who have not yet done so plan to do that in the future. Many residents wrote on their surveys that they are anxiously awaiting the arrival of a grocery store and restaurants and said they would visit them regularly.

Based on our results, residents of New Urbana walk in their neighborhood significantly more than Southwood Estates residents and they rated the availability of nearby parks and playgrounds significantly higher than Southwood Estates residents. Though compared to Southwood Estates, New Urbana has more available neighborhood amenities such as parks, playgrounds, and other social meeting spaces and this may be the reason for the greater frequency of walking in the neighborhood. Because the new urban community provides more opportunities for social interaction it is not surprising that residents of New Urbana display a stronger sense of community than residents of the conventional suburban neighborhood examined here.

There were no significant differences demographically between the neighborhoods except the length of time residents have lived in the neighborhood, with Southwood Estates residents living in their neighborhood significantly longer than New Urbana residents. Southwood Estates is an older and more established neighborhood, so it would be expected that residents have lived there longer, as was the case. However, even if one would expect that in a longer-established neighborhood residents would have stronger social ties and a better developed sense of community, that was not the case, suggesting that the new urbanist features positively impacted the social aspects of the community life. Overall, there are a number of significant differences between the two neighborhoods on various social dimensions of residents' quality of life. New Urbana residents appear to feel a stronger sense of community with their neighbors, which may be due to their more frequent social interactions and greater participation in neighborhood activities, facts made possible by the new urban design.

Study Limitations and Recommendations

As with most neighborhood studies, probably the greatest limitation of our findings is the threat of self-selection bias. We cannot be sure that interneighborhood differences are solely a result of environmental differences between the two communities. Yet, the only significant demographic inter-group difference was that the suburban residents had lived in their community much longer. Although residents of the conventional development should have had a *stronger* sense of community, stronger social ties were identified in the neighborhood whose residents had a much shorter tenure. However, it is possible that residents of the New Urban development moved there in part because they are more community-minded. As Audirac (1999) has found, not all suburban residents are willing to sacrifice larger yards for proximity to shared neighborhood amenities, but some are.[18] We also recommend that post-occupancy research be conducted after all of the neighborhood businesses have opened, as their presence may promote more walking and social interaction, which may lead to changes in sense of community and more significant improvements in one's quality of life. The finding in the self-selection analysis related to walking behavior may be influenced by the opening of more neighborhood businesses, since those residents who do not walk as frequently might begin to do so once businesses will open.

The relatively small number of study participants and the modest response rate in each neighborhood are additional limitations of this work. When only a small percentage of residents are surveyed the sample may not be representative of the population under study (i.e., there may be significant differences between those residents who participated and those who did not respond). Yet, despite the limited sample size, the fact that there were several statistically significant differences between the two neighborhoods on various aspects of quality of life is noteworthy. Results also suggest that with a larger sample, possibly more inter-group differences may be identified. In general, it should be stressed that despite their shorter tenure, residents of the new urbanist development feel a stronger sense of community with their neighbors, which may be largely due to the unique characteristics of the new urban place that facilitate more frequent social interactions and greater participation in neighborhood activities.

Notes

1. See P. Calthorpe, *The Next American Metropolis: Ecology, Community, and the American Dream* (PrincetonNJ: Princeton Architectural Press, 1994); P. Katz, *The New Urbanism: Toward an Architecture of Community* (New York: McGraw-Hill, 1994); E. Talen, "Measuring the Public Realm: A Preliminary Assessment of the Link Between Public Space and Sense of Community," *Journal of Architectural and Planning Research* 17, no. 4 (2000): 344-360.

2. See M. Levine, D. D. Perkins, and D. V. Perkins, *Principles of Community Psychology: Perspectives and Applications,* 3rd ed., (New York: Oxford University Press, 2005); H. Lund, "Pedestrian Environments and Sense of Community," *Journal of Planning Education and Research* 21, no. 3 (2002): 301-312.

3. Listed here are some of the works that discuss the importance of social interaction as a mediator in the creation of a "sense of community": J. Jacobs, *The Death and Life of Great American Cities* (New York: Random House, 1961); L. Demerath and D. Levinger,

"The Social Qualities of Being on Foot: A Theoretical Analysis of Pedestrian Activity, Community, and Culture," *City & Community*, 2, no. 3 (2003): 217-237; F. E. Kuo, W.C. Sullivan, R. L. Coley, and L. Brunson, "Fertile Ground for Community: Inner-City Neighborhood Common Spaces," *American Journal of Community Psychology*, 26, no. 6 (1998): 823-851.

4. J. M. Plas and S. E. Lewis, "Environmental Factors and Sense of Community in a Planned Town," *American Journal of Community Psychology* 24, no. 1 (1996): 109-114.

5. B. B. Brown and V. R. Cropper, "New Urban and Standard Suburban Subdivisions: Evaluating Psychological and Social Goals,"*Journal of the American Planning Association* 67, no. 4 (2001): 402-420.

6. J. Kim and R. Kaplan, "Physical and Psychological Factors in Sense of Community: New Urbanist Kentlands and Nearby Orchard Village,"*Environment and Behavior* 36, no. 3 (2004): 313-340.

7. J. Nasar and D. A. Julian, "The Psychological Sense of Community in the Neighborhood,"*Journal of the American Planning Association* 61, no. 2 (1995): 178-184.

8. L. Freeman, "The Effects of Sprawl on Neighborhood Social Ties,"*Journal of the American Planning Association* 67, no. 1(2001): 69-77.

9. Lund, *op. cit.*

10.O. Skjaeveland, "Effects of Street Parks on Social Interactions Among Neighbors: A Place Perspective,"*Journal of Architectural and Planning Research* 18, no. 2 (2001): 131-147.

11. Kuo, Sullivan, Coley, and Brunson, *op. cit.*

12. See Kim & Kaplan, *op. cit.*; Nasar & Julian, *op. cit.*; Lund, *op. cit.*; Kuo et al., *op. cit.*

13. Freeman, *op. cit.*

14. Skjaeveland, *op. cit.*

15. Brown & Cropper, *op. cit.*

16. New Urbana Neighborhood Resident, interview by John W. Vick, 2008.

17. D. Harvey, "The New Urbanism and the Communitarian Trap,"*Harvard Design Magazine,* Winter/Spring 1997: 1-3.

18. I. Audirac, "Stated Preference for Pedestrian Proximity: An Assessment of New Urbanist Sense of Community,"*Journal of Planning Education and Research* 19, no. 1 (1999): 53-66.

Chapter Nine

Best Businesses for New Urbanism Communities

Karl Besel

The success rates for businesses and nonprofits vary greatly according to a number of factors, including location, industry and experience of business owners.[1] However, many studies have found that broadly speaking, about one-half of businesses survive to their fifth year.[2] It's worth noting that this number tends to increase with the number of workers a firm employs,[3] meaning that success rates for smaller businesses are typically lower than those of their larger counterparts. While studies that examine business success often vary as a result of the academic field of the researcher, a fairly common theme across scholarly disciplines is the key role played by management in business survival rates.Subsequently, most studies, regardless of the academic discipline of the researchers, show that organizations that are run by experienced managers exhibit the highest survival rates.[4]

The numerous obstacles faced by new businesses are compounded when entrepreneurs attempt to initiate commercial ventures within underserved urban areas. Access to capital has been noted as a primary impediment to initiating these businesses by academics ranging from Wayne State University economist Timothy Bates to Harvard Business School professor Michael Porter. While both of these prominent academics have championed the need to invest within these communities for decades, Bates and Porter differ with regard to their views on the role of government in structuring commercial investment strategies. Porter's research on underserved areas has led him to conclude that inner cities typically exhibit assets such as access to warehouses, factories, as well as cheap and abundant labor supplies which gives them a "genuine competitive advantage."[5] Porter views artificial inducements in the form of government mandates and subsidies as impediments to the incubation of businesses within underserved areas. In contrast, Bates purports that Porter's competitive advantage theory oversimplifies the commercial dilemmas of inner cities, and subsequently race continues to an issue in access to capital. Bates' research includes comprehensive studies statistically controlling for credit and other risk factors. In light of the continuing problems related to racial discrimination within underserved areas, as well as a general unwillingness of the private sector to invest within the inner city, Bates concludes that private action needs to be supported by government invention.[6] In tandem with Bates' analyses of inner city commercial activities, Rubin's recent study (2012) of underserved areas builds a compelling case for why the public sector needs to take a leading role in creating an environment to stimulate private investment. [7]

While urban scholars have argued about the best strategies for small business development for decades, little is known about what businesses are best suited for new urbanism communities. Subsequently, interviews conducted with developers and city officials alike as a part of this study showed that the dearth of information available on new urbanist businesses made designing the commercial sector more problematic than the residential side of communities. This virtual absence of market analysis research was evident within both suburban and urban redevelopment sites.[8] Since mixed use development is a key component of neotraditionalism, it makes sense that developers, city officials, and entrepreneurs would want information on the track records of businesses that decide to establish commercial ventures within these types of communities. The following comparative case study provides detailed analysis on how businesses are faring within five suburban and urban communities. In addition to examining differences and commonalities between these distinct neighborhoods, the authors also attempted to make comparisons between neighborhoods with differing socioeconomic characteristics.

The Setting

Tables 9.1 and 9.2 provide demographic information about each of five communities selected for this study. The authors selected two suburban communities (Village of West Clay, Norton Commons, and Celebration) as well as two urban redevelopment neighborhoods (Park DuValle and Duneland Village. Both of the newer suburban developments (Village of West Clay and Norton Commons) are located just outside of their respective states' largest metropolitan areas (Indianapolis and Louisville) within the suburbs of Carmel, Indiana, and Prospect, Kentucky,respectively.Duneland Village is located within the greater Gary metropolitan area, and Park DuValle is situated on the Westside of Louisville. Both of these redevelopment communities were formerly housing projects that were razed in order to make room for Hope VI funded neotraditional neighborhoods. While all four of these communities were initiated between 2000 and 2004 and subsequently exhibit similar neighborhood population (ranging between 5,015 and 7,630), Celebration is the oldest of the communities selected, with the first residents moving into their traditionally designed homes in 1996. This highly developed Orlando based development exhibits the largest population by far of the five neighborhoods at 8,780 residents in 2010. Celebration in many ways is in a category unto itself with its cutting edge school system and related neighborhood based amenities that has been the subject of critically acclaimed books such as Naisbitt's (1999) *High Tech, High Touch* novel about the intersection between technological innovation and increased demands for human interaction.[9] This well knownneotraditional community is included within this examination so that comparisons can be made between this well resourced "experimental" community heavily financed by the

Disney Corporation and new urbanist developments which followed Celebration which had no choice but to slowly build their commercial sectors.

Table 9.1: Income Data for Selected New Urbanist Communities

Income Data by Census Tract	2000 Median Family Income	2010 Estimated Median Family Income	Percent Change in Median Family Income
Village West Clay	138,897	172,162	23.95%
Celebration	54,832	69,785	27.27%
Norton Commons	118,629	148,703	25.35%
Park DuValle	27,597	34,593	25.35%
Duneland Village	37,902	46,622	23.01%

Source: *Federal Financial Institutions Examinations Council 2010 Summary Census Demographic Information*

Table 9.2: Selected Community Demographics, 2010

Demographics by Census Tract	Census Tract(s) Population	Percent Below Poverty Line	Percent Minority
Village West Clay	6,701	1.39%	8.89%
Celebration	8,780	10.06%	22.80%
Norton Commons	5,015	1.48%	8.49%
Park DuValle	7,630	28.04%	98.55%
Duneland Village	6,432	21.99%	84.97%

Source: *Federal Financial Institutions Examinations Council 2010 Summary Census Demographic Information*

The Study

Data were gathered primarily from census data reports and interviews with key informants. These interviewees consisted of professionals that played crucial roles in the establishment and growth of each of the five communities examined within this study. Informants interviewed as a part of this project included developers, architects, community business owners, realtors, public officials, and original residents. Efforts were made to select informants from each of the neighborhoods. A total of 15 individuals were interviewed beginning during the summer of 2009, and concluding over the spring of 2011. In addition to the use of census data reports and notes from these interviews, the authors also utilized community and business websites to collect data on businesses. Tables 9.3 and 9.4 show community based businesses that have been in operation for at least five years, as well as businesses that have closed. The authors constructed seven (7)classifications for neighborhood businesses which included the following: 1) beauty and barber shops; 2) wellness (i.e., gyms, spas), 3) education and human services; 4) health care (i.e., medical physicians, health clinics, and hospitals); 5) professional and financial services (i.e., insurance agencies, architects, and financial/tax services) 6) general retail (i.e., clothing stores, wedding boutiques); and 7) restaurants and grocery stores. Some businesses which were unique to their particular community and subsequently did not readily fit into any of the categories included Celebration's movie theater. As the "new urbanism gone wild" development within this study, Celebration is able to support a unique arrayment of establishments not found within any of the other communities, including a movie theater, an electric car dealership, a jewelry store, as well as a hotel. In addition, some governmental entities such as the Louisville Water Company, are not included within these figures. These tables also do not capture thevarying locations of these businesses, especially when suburban neighborhoods are compared to the urban redevelopment ones. Neither of the redevelopment communities have been able to successfully attract businesses to "open shop" within their residential sector. Nonetheless, they have been able to catalyze business development within a fifteen minute walk of their neighborhood residents. Despite these limitations in accurately portraying the growth and nature of commercial development within these communities, these charts depict several patterns in business viability. These patterns include relatively high business closure rate for restaurants and grocery stores within all of the neighborhoods.

Key informant interviews revealed three themes that provide insight into reasons for these closures, including visibility and access problems, price of goods, and lack of patronage by local residents. Village of West Clay developer TomHuston stated "it's difficult for many of our businesses to make it if they are not located on a main fairway. The exception to this rule would be Helen Wells (a West Clay modeling agency). Her business has a lot of name recognition, so it doesn't matter that this agency is located right in the center of the Village."[10]

Huston's viewpoint was echoed by several of the interviewees, who often noted that "the perimeter of the development" is the best place to locate businesses that typically need high levels of visibility and access, such as restaurants, grocery stores, and general retail shops.

Table 9.3: Open Businesses

Business Type	Village WC	Celebration	Park DuValle	Norton Commons	Duneland Village
Barber/Beauty Salons	1	0	2	2	0
Wellness	0	0	0	1	0
Education/Human Services	2	2	0	1	0
Health Care	2	3	0	1	1
Professional/ Financial Services	17	23	1	8	5
Retail	6	4	1	2	2
Restaurants/ Grocery Stores	1	7	2	5	0

Table 9.4: Closed Businesses

Business Type	Village WC	Celebration	Park DuValle	Norton Commons	Duneland Village
Wellness	1	0	0	0	0
Education/Human Services	0	0	0	0	1
Health Care	0	0	0	0	1
Retail	0	2	0	0	1
Restaurants/ Grocery Stores	1	3	1	1	2

Lisa Baird, one of the first residents in Celebration, captured the sentiments of many of the key informants with regard to price of goods sold within grocery and retail stores. "People spend a lot on their homes, but we'll still go to Wal-Mart if grocery items are too expensive. Price is just as important to residents as convenience," quipped Baird in reference to a grocery store that went out of business with Celebration.[11] Lastly, interviewees from all of the communities frequently stressed the importance of attracting and maintaining the patronage of local residents. This viewpoint was evident even within Celebration which is frequented by a lot of tourists as a result of its close proximity to Disneyworld. "Many of the restaurants that have closed within Celebration were ones that never appealed to the locals. These businesses need to appeal to both local and tourists alike," stated lifetime resident and doctoral student Drew Baird.[12]

Table 9.3 shows that professional and financial services exhibit the highest levels of business viability. While these types of establishments were more prevalent within the suburban communities, the two redevelopment neighborhoods have been able to successfully attract and retain tax services, such as H & R Block, as well as insurance agencies. In addition to professional and financial services, health care establishments ranging from hospitals and retirement homes to dermatologists and dentists have fared well over the past five years within all of the communities. In many cases, such as the Park DuValle Health Clinic, these agencies are nonprofit. It is also significant to note that these businesses were generally the biggest employers found within the neighborhoods examined, especially the retirement homes and hospitals that operate within Park DuValle, Village of West Clay, and Celebration respectively. Nonprofit and governmental agencies were not limited to just medical establishments within these developments. Most of the communities have been able to support at least educational entity, varying from the preschool found within Norton Commons to the elementary and secondary schools supported by the residents of Celebration. In tandem with the "village within the city" type of neighborhoods admired by Lewis Mumford, all of these communities, regardless of their varying median family incomes, have been able to support a diverse mix of proprietary businesses, nonprofit agencies, and governmental institutions.

Dilemmas in Planning Commercial Sites

Two of the more pervasive planning dilemmas encountered by the developers within these communities pertained to market analysis reports and the parking needs of many business owners. With regard to the market analysis reports, the former Director of Development for the Village of Clay Jose Kruetz stated "We had nothing to go on as far as market reports that informed us about businesses for this type of neighborhood. We conducted our own focus groups to figure out what residents wanted for their homes and neighborhood amenities, but we had nothing for the commercial side."[13] In addition to this viewpoint that was shared by many of Kruetz's counterparts within the other suburban communities, development directors for the urban neighborhood often found that the limited number of market analysis reports available to themprovided recommendations that ran counter to the objectives for the community. "A market analysis generated for Park DuValle showed that this neighborhood would be a good place to locate a liquor store. Because of the stigma attached with this type of business, and negative connotation within the community, we weren't going to do this," stated Willie Jones, Vice President of the Community Builders Development Corporation.[14] In general, the most pressingchallenge in building the commercial sector within both of the redevelopment communities examined related to fighting against the "crime ridden" neighborhood image. Development directors for both Duneland Village and Park DuValle were very cognizant of this negative perception, and subsequently worked to induce businesses with a more positive image so that other businesses would be more likely to follow. Parking issues were considered secondary concerns in nature to dilemmas with marketing reports (or lack thereof). Nonetheless, most of the key informants involved in planning the commercial sectors reported that some businesses were reluctant to open shop within a new urbanist community as a result of the lack of parking spaces available to their prospective customers. In many ways this concern is a double edged sword; one of the most appealing aspects of living in a neotraditional community for many residents is the emphasis placed on walking and biking. It's logistically difficult, as well as not being favorable to most residents, to develop ample parking spaces for a limited number of potential businesses that may desire this "amenity." Essentially, this so called amenity to some businesses is an eyesore to many residents that select to live within a new urbanist community. Fortunately all of the communitiesexamined feature neighborhood plans that favor the pedestrian and the resident over the motorized vehicle.

Independent Business vs. Chains

In tandem with the "village within the city" ideal traditional town developers aspire to attain, key informants interviewed were generally more amenable to independently owned businesses locating within or in close proximity to their particular community. That being said, individuals involved in the fostering of business growth within the redevelopment communities examined spoke in very favorable terms about corporately owned businesses selecting their neighborhood for commercial activity. Subsequently, Community Builder's Willie Jones spoke invery favorable terms about Kentucky Fried Chicken opening a restaurant a block away from Park DuValle. "This neighborhood has not been able to support any businesses for a long time since it was too crime ridden. Now that the crime rate has gone down since the Villages of Park DuValle were built, they want to locate here," stated Jones.[15] In light of past problems with fostering any sort of legal commercial venture within the two redevelopment sites examined, it's no wonder that debate over the virtues of independent businesses over corporate ones is virtually nonexistent. What is more surprising is the prevalence of corporately owned businesses within the suburban neighborhoods included within this study. The closing of a locally owned coffee shop only to be replaced by a Starbucks, as well as the imposing presence of a Morgan Stanley office and a Marriott hotel (yes, the Bohemian Hotel is ironically owned by Marriott), indicate that"Corporate America" is alive and well in Celebration. This growing presence of Corporate America at the expense of a shrinking number of independently or locally owned in Celebration prompted a colleague of mine to refer to this Disney community as "Celabation." This absence of sex appealmy colleague found in Celebration as a result of the growing presence of commercial chains is also evident within communities such as the Village of West Clay, where the planned opening of a CVS pharmacy in the neighborhood "forced" the neighborhood grocery store out of business, according to this store's former owner. While my colleague may beg to differ, chains and independents can coexist within new urbanist communities, as witnessed by the intermingling of locally owned and corporate entities within historic neighborhoods for decades. Subsequently, neighborhood planning and local zoning boards have ensured that these chains conform to traditional design patterns. For example, the West Clay CVS is designed in art deco style, and actually looks more like an old movie theater than a bland suburban pharmacy. Celebration's Bohemian Hotel, as an example of Marriot's new "signature line" hotels, looks more like a vintage downtown hotel than your typical strip mall Marriot. If anything, corporately owned businesses possess greater resources and subsequently are more apt to take a risk by investing within a new urbanist community than many local entrepreneurs, especially in a lackluster economy. Thus, a certain number of chain businesses within neotraditionalcommunities may actually enhance the vibrancy of commercial activity.

Conclusion

A thriving commercial sector is an essential component of any neotraditional community. Like the myriad of stores, shops, and taverns that have been a part of both rural and urban communities for overmillennia, new urbanist developments need to foster sustainable climates for business. The dearth of studies and subsequent market reports available to developers and public officials alike to design and plan commercial sectors for neotraditional communities has made this process difficult for individuals such as the ones interviewed for this study, who have attempted to cultivate vibrant commercial sectors within their developments. This analysis of five new urbanist communities, while limited in scope, seeks to provide much needed insight and recommendations for fostering successful business climates within traditionally planned neighborhoods. In general, all of the communities examined have been able to build viable commercial sectors, whether they consist of redevelopment sites, or new suburban developments. This study shows that professional and financial services, as well as medical establishments,exhibit the highest success rates within these communities. Unfortunately, it appears from our analysis that redevelopment sites may only be able to sustain a limited number of the former types of businesses. In tandem with previous studies that address challenges encountered by inner city areas with regard to accessing capital for commercial ventures (e.g., Bates, Porter, Rubin), this study also found that similar to other businesses operating within underserved areas, access to capital is a central problem for business development within redevelopment sites. In building upon the work of both Bates (1997) and Rubin (2012), this analysis found that the public sector, in the form of governmentally funded nonprofit development corporations, tax incentives, as well as other types of public institutions, resources, and inducements, played a pivotal role in the creation of commercial sectors within both redevelopment sites examined.

Despite the relatively greater impediments encountered by commercial operations within these two redevelopment sites, this study found that certain types of businesses were less likely to sustain their operations, regardless of their service area.Subsequently, businesses that possess lower survival rates, such as restaurants and grocery stores, need to consider issues such as visibility and access in their marketing strategies, as well as aggressively catering to local residents. This appears to be the case for business owners within both suburban and redevelopment communities. In addition to proprietary businesses, commercial sector planners need to consider market demand for nonprofit health care, wellness and educational entities. Like medieval villages that sustained intergenerational populations while existing in relative isolation from neighboring towns, these agencies can provide services to young families and aging adults alike. In contrast to conventional suburbs whose sole focus is the young family, neotraditional developments feature a diverse array of businesses and services for residents of all stages of life. This study shows that retirement homes and a wide range of health care related businesses and nonprofits are a viable part of neotraditional communities, regardless of the neighborhood's median family income. In sum, cradle to grave services can and should be provided to residents within traditionally planned communities through a rich mix of propriety, nonprofit, and governmental entities.

Notes

1. Audretsch, D. (1992). Reviews.*Kyklos*, *45*(2), 294. Retrieved from Academic Search Premier database.
2. B.A. Kirchoff, Entrepreneurship and Dynamic Capitalism.(Westport, CT: Praeger, 1994).
3. B. D. Phillips and B.A. Kirchoff, "Formation, Growth, and Survival: Small Firm Dynamicsin the U.S. Economy."*Small Business Economics,* Vol. 1, (1989) 65–74.
4. J. Brüderl, P. Preisendörfer, and R. Ziegler, "Survival Chances of Newly Founded Business Organizations,"*American Sociological Review*, Vol. *57*, No 2, (1992) 227-242. Retrieved from Academic Search Premier database.
5. M.E. Porter, "The Competitive Advantage of the Inner City,"*Harvard Business Review*, May-June, (1995). 55-71. Retrieved from Academic Search Premier database.
6. T. Bates, "Michael Porter's Conservative Urban Agenda Will Not Revitalize America's Inner Cities: What Will?,"*Economic Development Quarterly*, Vol. 11 (1997). 39-54. Retrieved from Academic Search Premier database.
7. T.S. Rubin, "Countering the Rhetoric of Emerging Domestic Markets: Why More Information Alone Will Not Address the Capital Needs of Underserved Areas,"*Economic Development Quarterly,* Vol. 25, No. 2, (2012) 182-192. Retrieved from Academic Search Premier database.
8. Tom Huston and Willie Jones, interviews by Dr. Karl Besel, 2009.
9. J.Naisbitt, High Tech, High Touch, (New York: Broadway Books, 1999).
10. Tom Huston, *op. cit.*
11. Lisa Baird, interview by Dr. Karl Besel, 2011.
12. Drew Baird, interview by Dr. Karl Besel, 2011.
13. Jose Kruetz, interview by Dr. Karl Besel, 2009.
14. Willie Jones, interview by Dr. Karl Besel, 2009.
15. Willie Jones, *op. cit.*

Chapter Ten

Conclusion: Old and New Rules

Karl Besel and Viviana Andreescu

As mentioned in the introductory part of this manuscript, this book's main intention was to contribute to the literature on new urbanism by evaluating the socio-economic performance of several new urbanism developments by examining the public response to neotraditional communities and by highlighting some of the challenges faced by those who embraced the new urban design movement. Although the case studies included in this book do not constitute a representative sample of the new urbanist communities currently existing in the United States (e.g., in 2002, a survey of the new urbanist projects identified 472 neighborhood-scale projects either built, under construction, or in planning in United States),[1] our findings may be used in future systematic studies that would examine in more detail how successful the design and planning strategies grounded in traditional urban forms actually are.

"The new urbanism has been variously dismissed as a reflection of middle-class nostalgia, a cover for class warfare, and a symptomatic manifestation of postmodern culture. It has been subjected to surprisingly superficial criticism, too often based on the way particular projects have been represented in the press, on marketing materials taken at face value, or on the rhetorical excesses of practitioners."[2] Approximately a decade ago, Cliff Ellis, a professor of urban planning, addressed and responded to the main criticisms directed at new urbanism projects. The author noted that the debate around new urbanism could be broken into three interrelated areas — empirical performance, ideological and cultural issues (e.g., proper role of historical pattern in city planning; the importance of public realm that reinforces social interaction; political implications of different urban forms, etc), and aesthetic quality of the projects. As Ellis observed, the new urbanists' empirical claims regarding the superiority of the neotraditional design with respect to trip reduction, infrastructure costs, environmental protection, and housing affordability continue to be discussed.[3] We may add that controversies regarding the new urbanists' ways of addressing ideological, cultural, and aesthetic issues in planning and design do exist and will continue to exist, as well.

Ambe Njoh (2009: 8) acknowledged that although new urbanist projects are frequently appraised based on their physical design, the main goals of the new urbanist movement, as stipulated in the Congress of New Urbanism's Charter, are to create developments that would ensure economic viability, social development, social equity, common welfare, and physical and spatial functioning.[4] Summarizing the information included in the case studies presented in this book, we will try to determine to what extent these objectives have been attained, referring solely to the new urbanist developments that served as data sources for the present research.

The *economic objectives* of the new urbanists refer to the viability and financial sustainability of the projects they coordinate. They also refer to the ability of the projects to generate employment opportunities for the residents who decide to live in the newly developed areas. Additionally, the third level of judging the economic performance of a new urbanist development refers to housing affordability.[5] We consider that an important aspect that should be also discussed when the economic performance of a project is evaluated refers to the business activity in the new urbanist communities. Based on the analyses included in this book, it could be concluded that the new urbanists' economic goals as pertaining only to the projects presented here have been partially attained.

Although the individual total costs of the projects examined (e.g., Park DuValle in Kentucky; West Clay in Indiana; Haile Plantation and Town of Tioga in Florida; New Urbana in Tennessee) are only partially reported here (i.e., a $220,000,000 investment of public and private funds was secured for the Park DuValle project) and specific economic information regarding employment opportunities for the new residents is missing, based on the public's relatively high willingness to take up residence in neighborhoods such as Park DuValle in Louisville, Kentucky (where public demand for housing exceeded the expectations[6] and where there were people on waiting lists), the new urbanist community in Tennessee, or West Clay, in Indianapolis, Indiana, it could be concluded that, at least in these three cases, the economic ventures appeared to be worthwhile.

Regarding housing affordability, our analysis produced mixed results. Currently, the newly developed area in Park DuValle, Louisville, Kentucky includes over 1,000 mixed-income rental and homeownership housing units. Even if the large majority of new housing units available for renting had been provided at market rates, the average cost of the replacement housing units was $160,000, a housing price usually paid in late 1990s (when the first houses became available for sale) in upper-middle class neighborhoods in Louisville.[7] However, it should be noted that in 2006, housing prices for single-family homes for sale at the time varied from $81,000 to $250,000. At the end of 2005, there were completed 255 houses with 25 more under construction. The majority of the owners were first-time homebuyers and 55 percent of the houses went to households earning less than eighty percent of the area's median income.[8] Nevertheless, at the time of this writing, 53 of the newly built houses are for sale, with prices varying from $24,500 to $218,665; most of them (83 percent) are foreclosure (35) and pre-foreclosure (9) sales.[9]

The case studies that focused on two new urbanist communities in Florida (Haile Plantation and the Town of Tioga) indicated that the residents targeted by developers in these areas were more likely to be middle- and upper-middle class individuals. Although the housing prices in both communities varied, the lowest housing price was approximately $150,000, suggesting that those who could afford to purchase housing in the new urbanist developments were relatively better-off individuals in terms of disposable income. The Village of West Clay in Indiana is a predominantly Caucasian bedroom community, whose residents have among the highest median family income (i.e., $170,000) within the state. However, even if the new urbanist community presented in this book continues to be perceived as an exclusive community, taking into account the variations in housing prices (from $60,000 to $3,000,000) and the diversity of housing units (i.e., the West Clay development includes apartment buildings, townhomes, and single-family homes), it seems that the development succeeded to attract people from different income levels.

Ellis (2002: 269) contended that, in general, "the commercial components of new urbanist projects have been the most difficult elements to complete."[10] Nonetheless, the authors of the book chapter that examined the business sectors in five new urbanist communities (Park DuValle and Norton Commons in Kentucky; West Clay and Duneland in Indiana; Celebration in Florida) concluded that all these communities had viable commercial sectors. The analysis also showed that the establishments that seemed to dominate the business environments in the study locations offered financial and professional services (e.g., banks, insurance agencies, etc). These institutions represented approximately 51% of the total number (N=106) of businesses open in the five study areas at the time the data were collected. Although not too many businesses (N=14) had to close their operations in the study areas, more than half of them were restaurants and grocery stores. Regarding the business activity in the new urbanist suburban developments in Florida, the researchers concluded that business activity in Haile Plantation Center, where 40 businesses currently operate providing a variety of services, is viable as well.

However, as presented in one of the case studies, the vice president of Community Builders, the group awarded the contract to redevelop Park DuValle in Louisville, acknowledged that the least successful part of the revitalization project was the ability to activate a commercial zone with a lot of retail capacity. Out of eight businesses the area hosts, there are only one general retail store, one restaurant, and one grocery store. A similar lack of diversity of services was found in Duneland Village, located within the Gary metropolitan area in Indiana. At the same time, it should be mentioned that when compared to suburban developments, commercial areas in infill projects are at disadvantage due to space constraints that limit the area available for construction and parking.

The exploratory analysis presented in this book suggests that business survival in neotraditional developments remains a sensitive topic for new urbanists. Business failure may be caused by excessive regulations, high interest rates, dysfunctional management, operational inefficiencies, insufficient marketability, inability to compete with similar businesses, lack of public demand for the goods and services offered, and/or a declining market. Nevertheless, additional research is needed to determine the specific causes of business failure, to recognize the potential opportunities that would create a viable economic development, and to formulate pertinent recommendations that would contribute effectively to the business success in new urbanist developments.

As Brain (2005: 218) noted, "although generally design-centered, the new urbanism has encompassed a complex social agenda, only partly explicit in its rhetoric." [11] In short, the *social goals* of new urbanism are to produce environments that would increase the residents' sense of community and would favor social interactions; to generate urban spaces that would create equitable access to resources and opportunities; and, to increase the quality of life of all the residents. [12] The quantitative analysis that compared one conventional community to a new urbanist community from Tennessee in terms of residential satisfaction, housing satisfaction, and people's sense of community showed that residents of the new urbanist development expressed a significantly higher sense of community, interacted more often with their neighbors, and participated in neighborhood activities more frequently than the residents of the traditionally developed neighborhood. However, the researchers noted that the new urbanist community in Tennessee lacked racial, religious, and economic diversity, an issue found problematic by some of the interviewed residents.

Even if a comparison basis was not provided, interviews conducted with residents living in the new urbanist communities in Florida (Haile Plantation and Town of Tioga) indicated that the study participants from the newly developed areas are highly satisfied with their communities and that they perceive the new neighborhoods as being characterized by a high sense of neighborliness. In addition, the examined communities in Florida, West Clay in Indiana, and the new urbanist community in Tennessee have been built in a way that stimulates walking and bicycling, contributing not only to a decrease reliance on the automobile, but also to the public health.

Yet, in the Park DuValle neighborhood, without forgetting that the revitalization project had several positive consequences, such as significant reduction in crime, a 1990-2008 six-time increase in the average household medium income, better quality housing, and more amenities, it should be noted that once the development was created, the new rental units available to low-income residents diminished almost by half. In addition, another recent evaluation study of the Park DuValle project found that only 25 percent of the persons currently living in public housing in the area had an improved quality of life and that 75 percent of the low-income residents were left without upgraded HOPE VI homes or without homes at all and have been displaced. [13] In about two decades, the population in the area decreased by 3,000 people (from 4,347 in 1990 to 1,355 in 2008) and the community remained racially segregated (i.e., about 98 percent of the new residents are African Americans). Although limited, our research findings suggests that the neotraditional development projects examined in this book have not succeeded to fully satisfy the social goals formulated by new urbanists. Despite the fact that public satisfaction toward the new environment and a more developed sense of community were recorded in most cases, there are still issues related to social equity, racial diversity, true income mixture, and common welfare that remained unsolved.

New urbanism proponents tend to consider convenience and aesthetic appeal as being the main attributes of urban design.[14] However, new urbanists also recognize that form and function in space are not independent.[15] In general, referring to the findings from the case studies included in this book and based on the residents' perceptions, our evaluation of the new urbanist projects' ability to ensure *physical and spatial functioning* is positive.

Residents from the new urbanist community in Tennessee frequently praised the architectural features of the buildings. Compared to the residents from the conventionally developed suburban area, residents of the new urbanist development rated significantly higher the availability of nearby parks and playgrounds, factors that encourage social interaction and contribute to the residents' general wellbeing.

As stated previously in this book, the goal of the Park DuValle HOPE VI Plan was to transform a public housing neighborhood into a mixed-income neighborhood with rental and homeownership opportunities for a wide range of income groups. In order to create a mixed-income pattern, rental and homeownership units alternate throughout the community on a street-by-street basis. No distinction is made between subsidized and market-rate rental units. The mix manages to create the look and feel of a traditional neighborhood in which there are a variety of house sizes. The architectural character of the houses, codified in a pattern book, follows Louisville traditions (i.e., the architectural styles used here are Craftsman, Victorian, and Colonial Revival) and the configuration and design of streets and parks directly continue the forms established in Louisville by F. L. Olmsted, the famous American landscape designer. In order to create 'good blocks', the streets and park ways are lined with closely spaced houses with front doors, porches, and windows facing the street, thus creating a neighborhood space. The exterior design of homes and apartments incorporates "defensible space" features (e.g., raised porches, large windows) that promote safety and security. The backyards are served by alleys for parking and service. A clear distinction is made between public and private areas. The neighborhood has narrow streets to discourage excessive automobile usage, increase public safety, and encourage walking and social interaction. To accommodate the infrastructure needs of an inner-city development, the builder worked with Louisville Gas & Electric to modify easement requirements. In order to increase the curb appeal, all utilities were placed underground and in the rear of the units. In accordance with new urbanism design requirements, the development includes a Town Center that features healthcare facilities, shopping, dining, laundry services, and access to mass transit. Senior housing was placed around the development's Town Center, allowing seniors easier access to retail locations. Other notable amenities include an on-site elementary school, a community center, and two large parks with an Olympic-size swimming pool. Among the services offered to residents there are neighborhood-based employment and homeownership workshops. Residents have easy access to the town center, where most service and retail establishments were built. In 2000, the architect firm (Urban Design Associates) commissioned to plan and design the Park DuValle neighborhood received the American Institute of Architects Honor Award for Regional and Urban Design.[16]

The other three new urbanist projects presented in this book that are developed in suburban areas in Florida (Haile Plantation and Town of Tioga) and Indiana (West Clay) also incorporate well new urbanism design features, such as traditional architectural styles and traditional design details, buildings close to the sidewalks, parking for residents located in the back of the lots, attractive landscaping, narrow streets to discourage intense traffic, town centers with office and retail buildings in walking distance from most neighborhoods in the developments, and numerous parks and green spaces.

Although the residents' participation and involvement in the designing and planning of their neighborhoods was limited in all the examined sites, based on our research findings it is safe to contend that the developments presented here managed to respond well to most of the residents' expectations, needs, and desires. It should be mentioned, however, that many of those who decided to live in the new urbanist communities were familiar with the characteristics of new urbanist developments and favored them over conventional suburban developments. As noted in one of the book chapters, residents who preferred new urbanist communities were appreciative of a vital community life and wanted to interact with neighbors, being less concerned about easy access to highways, large lots, or large-size homes, which were factors more likely to motivate house selection in typical suburban developments. These findings suggest that Americans' preferences for housing arrangements vary and that the new urbanists were able to appeal to a segment of the population that will probably grow in the future.

In conclusion, based on the research included in this book, although the neotraditional developments reviewed here managed to generate built environments that function well and are aesthetically pleasing, it seems that Susan Fainstein's[17] predictions regarding the success of the new urbanists' efforts to overcome social injustices continue to remain valid.

> The [new urbanists'] real problem replicates the one that defeated Ebenezer Howard's radical principles in the construction of garden cities. To achieve investor backing for his schemes, Howard was forced to trade away his aims of a socialist commonwealth and a city that accommodated all levels of society. The new urbanists must also rely on private developers to build and finance their vision; consequently, they are producing only slightly less exclusive neighborhoods than the ones they dislike. Although their creations will contain greater physical diversity than their predecessors, their social composition will not differ markedly.[18]

Old rules and new rules

Bill Maher's HBO show Real Time always features a final segment where Maher provides a provocative and often irreverent look at daily practices, fads, and trends that, in his opinion, need to change. The following section, while probably not as clever and savory as Maher's weekly rants, attempts to summarize the collective lessons emerging from this book and other studies that examined new urbanist communities. We propose some "New Rules" but also support keeping some of the "Old Rules" that continue to hold relevance within the post real estate crisis world. Our suggestions try to address some of the challenges new urbanism proponents are currently facing and include the following:

- *Establish a proper balance of professional expertise and community input*

The Congress of New Urbanism (CNU) Charter explicitly endorses a participatory approach to urban design and planning and acknowledges that community input should be solicited on a regular basis.[19] In this way, future and potential residents could be educated regarding design alternatives and the development plans would be able to better reflect local preferences. In addition, new urbanist developers should familiarize the public with the movement's main objectives.

We should add to this 'rule' that when commitments are made, developers should respect them or they should explain to the public why changes to the original plans have been made. For instance, as the case study focusing on neotraditional developments in Florida showed, the most recent developments in Haile Plantation had lesser new urbanist design features (e.g., sidewalks were very small or were missing; individual lots were much smaller) than the earlier developments, suggesting that once the public demand for a particular development increased, developers were more interested in maximizing profits than in following all the new urbanist design principles. Also, as of this writing, many of the current residents within Village of West Clay are protesting and some are even taking legal action against the developer of this new urbanism community within Carmel, Indiana. These residents contend that the developer's sale of neighborhood property to a production builder goes against the developer's initial agreement with the neighborhood association, which stated that custom homes to be built in the community will be consistent with certain "traditional" architectural styles. Considering the relatively cheaper price of the production homes that might negatively affect the property value of the homes already built in the area, the public discontent is not surprising. However, in situations like this, new urbanist developers could remind the public that one of the movement's goals is to provide affordable housing for mix-income populations.

Nonetheless, public resistance to change could be diminished if residents are better informed and educated with respect to the social objectives of the new urbanism movement. In support of their claims, new urbanist developers could also provide the public with concrete examples from older, more established neighborhoods that continue to be popular and can be found in any large or mid-size American city. As presented in this book, historical preservation neighborhoods such as Cherokee Triangle and Old Louisville in Louisville, Kentucky have demonstrated since their creation more than one century ago, that traditionally planned communities can support a wide variety of housing designs and types and can be still viable and in demand. Additionally, developers could present to the public the results of studies showing that homes within traditionally planned neighborhoods are typically wise investments. For instance, a study released in 2011 by the US Environmental Protection Agency (EPA) and based on 1998-2004 resale data from 18 smart growth developments and 18 conventional suburban developments in eight states from all US regions found that smart growth communities achieved higher residential sale prices and value per square foot than their conventional counterparts.[20] Leinberger (2011) also contended that if in the late 1990s, high-end outer suburbs contained most of the expensive housing in the United States, today, the most expensive housing can be found in high-density, pedestrian friendly gentrified neighborhoods of the center city and inner suburbs.[21] In addition, the neotraditional developments provide intangible benefits (such as an increased sense of community, increased safety, healthier environments, etc.) that are highly regarded by many Americans.

- *Consider demographic changes when assessing market demands for mixed-use developments*

Leinberger (2011) acknowledged that America is currently experiencing a profound structural shift with lasting consequences on real estate markets because of a major demographic event — the convergence of the two largest generations in the country's history, the baby boomers (born between 1946 and 1964) and the millennials (born between 1979 and 1996), which today represent half of the total population.[22] Economic concerns combined with the aging of the baby boomers and an increase in the number of single adults (both young and older) will continue to negatively affect public demand for conventional urban developments.[23] According to Kennedy (2010), the city of the future should be an age-friendly, vibrant intergenerational community, where the spectrum of senior housing options should be expended and the build environment should match each stage of life.[24]

As presented in this book, market demand studies have found that persons belonging to the fastest growing age group (i.e., individuals age 55 to 65) tend to prefer mixed-use developments over exclusively residential communities. A growing number of young families also prefer this type of development that offers several benefits, such as a greater housing variety and density, more affordable and life-cycle housing (e.g., starter homes, larger homes, senior housing), reduced distances between housing, workplaces, retail businesses and other amenities, pedestrian and bicycle-friendly environments, land-use synergy (i.e., residents become customers for retailers and retail businesses provide amenities for residents), and a stronger neighborhood character. For instance, according to a 2011 survey by the National Association of Realtors, many baby boomers, who are approaching retirement and want to downsize, declared they would like to live in a walkable urban downtown neighborhood, a suburban town center or a small town. For life style reasons or for not having to own a car, the millennials tend to prefer urban downtowns and suburban town centers, as well; "overall, only 12 percent of future homebuyers want the drivable suburban-fringe houses that are in such oversupply,"[25] while 58 percent of the surveyed homebuyers declared they would prefer mixed-used neighborhoods where one can easily walk to stores or other businesses.[26] Byproducts of the lifestyle fostered by mixed-use developments are not only the shorter commutes and increased accessibility via transit, which result in reduced transportation costs and contribute to the reduction of carbon emissions. They also include the reduced costs city and county governments have to pay on infrastructure and public services offered by police or fire departments.

Trend analysis for assessing market demand for residential and commercial development needs to become more reliant on the best sources for making demographic predictions, such as census data projections. In addition, consumer surveys conducted on representative samples could determine public preferences and could be used by new urbanism proponents to better estimate the market demand for the products offered by neotraditional developments.

- *Establish university partnerships to rebuild disadvantaged communities and reduce social inequalities*

One of the chapters included in this book focused on a university town in Florida and the role played by the university in the development of two neotraditional communities built on the urban fringe. Although no clear partnerships have been established in this case between the university and the developers, university employees were highly represented among the residents of the newly developed communities, developers consulted with faculty regarding planning details, and student interns participated in several stages of the project. We argue that partnerships between new urbanist developers and public institutions of higher education would be beneficial, especially when infill projects that plan to retrofit physically and obsolete inner-city neighborhoods are undertaken. As one scholar noted, there are over 3,500 higher institutions in the United States and those involved in the construction of new urbanist communities "need to access the brain power of colleges and universities in the United States not only to determine the economies and design of Americans' homes, but also to figure out strategies that would empower the lives of the poor."[27] We consider that through university partnerships, new urbanist developers could be able to offer a more suitable and convincing solution to social injustice issues that continue to remain unsolved in many urban areas.

*   *Find creative ways to stimulate the removal of zoning obstacles*

Recent public opinion polls indicate that since the beginning of the Obama administration, Americans have increasingly turned against the idea of "government regulation." According to a 2012 Pew Research Center survey, 52 percent of Americans believe that government regulation of business usually does more harm than good, while just 40 percent believe it is "necessary to protect the public interest." However, the overwhelming majority of Americans believe that government regulations of the food industry, car safety, workplace safety, prescription drugs, and even environmental protection should either be strengthened or be preserved as they are. Nonetheless, nearly 50 percent of Americans believe that small businesses are overregulated.[28]

Our country, probably more than any nation in the world, values freedom of action and favors efforts that provide minimal or no restrictions to individuals' activities and businesses alike. In our era of polarized politics, liberals and conservatives can often find common ground when it comes to enacting policies that support civil liberties and encourage free market competition. In addition, our opposing political parties typically favor policies that conform to our federalist model of government where state and local governments are allowed some level of discretion in implementing federal laws and policies.

With respect to neighborhood development or renewal, public officials and developers alike are often subjected to numerous rules and regulations before neighborhoods can be revitalized or new ones can be built. In the late 1990s, when criticized for contributing to the urban sprawl by building in suburbia instead of inner-city neighborhoods, A. Duany responded that he developed suburban areas because "better suburbs need to be built;" yet, Duany acknowledged that political opposition and obsolete zoning ordinances prevented him from working in inner cities.[29] Although Ellis noted that land-use separation and low densities are locked into zoning ordinances, mortgage financing requirements, and professional design standards, the author contended that this situation could gradually change.[30] Zoning that allows and even encourages mixed-use development is a standard feature of smart growth, which is advocated by new urbanists. Nowadays, however, most zoning boards continue to favor single-use developments and in most residential communities in Midwest and South, mixed-use developments are illegal.

Current Euclidian zoning regulations that affect the large majority of urban communities in United States should be revised not only because American cities deindustrialized and the need to separate residencies from hazardous factories ceased to exist, but mostly because single zoning is making the work-family balance more difficult to achieve, as greater distances need to be covered in order to integrate one's different life domains.[31] Lang and his colleagues

(2005) anticipated that even if over the next few years, many municipalities will adopt smart growth ordinances that will lower barriers to neighborhood retail in residential areas, many obstacles will persist. According to Lang et al. (2005), smart growth advocates should focus on reforming zoning regulations by attracting public support. For instance, "not-in-my-backyard" (NIMBY) opposition to mixed-use development might exist because most people justifiably object to big-box retail as a neighbor and to the associated traffic increase. But small-scale retail that fits into the neighborhood context should encounter less resistance, especially as such projects become more common and people find them to be a benefit rather than a detriment to their quality of life. In addition, new urbanists could use taxpayer strips as a model for a new generation of neighborhood retail strips that accommodate cars and pedestrians. Typically, suburban residents lack pedestrian access to the strip malls that are close to their residencies and must get on the highway to reach a store within sight of their home. "Shopping strips may prove a good place to test out variants on smart growth design. Redesigning them also could help reestablish an early 20th century urban design tradition, hybrid shopping strips."[32]

Since our Constitution grants specific powers to state governments but not to local ones, state assemblies need to take the lead in formulating new laws that favor mixed-use developments so that local zoning boards can be provided with new guidelines that support this practice. State governments also exhibit the constitutional authority to regulate, enforce, and initiate tax policies that may favor the growth and expansion of high density communities. For this reason some states such as Kentucky do not allow local governments to offer tax abatements, while in neighboring Indiana even small towns make frequent use of this controversial tax strategy.

Higher density mixed-used developments should be supported not only because they are vital and necessary for a healthy urban area, as Jane Jacobs[33] argued half a century ago, but also because they encourage a more efficient use of taxpayer dollars (e.g., they are reducing highway and related infrastructure costs and are reducing police and fire protection expenses). In light of cost savings, developers that build high density, mixed-use neighborhoods should be provided with more tax incentives than their counterparts who continue to foster uncontrolled urban sprawl. In the same time, as Lang et al. (2005) contended, supporters of smart growth and mixed-used developments should gather data and clear performance characteristics from existing new transit-oriented developments because such efforts have the potential to educate local leaders and consumers about the benefits of this form of development and may eventually increase the public support for well-integrated mixed-use projects.[34] Additionally, as Leinberger and Kavage (2007) suggested, the new urbanism proponents should use smart growth advocates, such as FutureWise, Transportation Choices Coalition, and other environmental groups and local activists, to educate the general population about the benefits of concentrated high-density mixed-use developments (e.g., their potential to curb sprawl, reduce greenhouse emissions, reduce oil-dependence, and increase the fiscal health of local governments).[35]

- *Uncover convincing strategies to finance mixed-use projects*

Leinberger (2001), acknowledged that proponents of progressive development (i.e., new urbanism or smart growth or sustainable development) "are constantly confronted by the difficulty of financing" because financial markets are by necessity conservative[36] and smart growth developments are considered "risky lending"[37] Although the statement was formulated more than one decade ago, when new urbanist developments lacked a long track record of successful projects, in a recently published article Leinberger (2012) contended that mixed-use developments continue to be perceived as "complex developments that still carry high risk and, as such, costly capital (both equity and debt financing)."[38] According to the author, the financial community continues to express reservations when it comes to financing progressive developments because traditionally, banks, investors, and Wall Street analysts have adhered to investment that reflects 19 standard product types.[39] Unfortunately, mixed-used development does not match any of these standardized real estate products. Overall, "the real estate finance industry lacks the experience, institutional mission or even fiduciary latitude to appropriately consider [mixed-use] development investments or loans."[40] However, despite legal and financial difficulties, new urbanism communities and mixed-use developments have been built and will continue to be built as long as market demand for them exists. Nonetheless, even if demand for more walkable, mixed-used neighborhoods is growing, due to challenges associated with financing, much of the demand remains unmet.[41]

Solutions to overcome present obstacles exist and there are scholarly research studies that address them. Lang and his colleagues, for example, made several pertinent recommendations that new urbanists should consider.

> Smart growth advocates need to set their sights on regulators of their financiers. The movement needs to better understand what will convince regulators, as well as investors, that these are good deals. (…) If smart growth advocates are, in fact, concerned with diversity in income, race, and ethnicity, then affordable housing has to be an essential part of the vision. Assuming performance is addressed, the inclusion of affordable housing also gains access to a number of potential regulatory and programmatic incentives from government. For instance, the Community Reinvestment Act (CRA) has been widely credited with improving capital flows to underserved neighborhoods and communities. Alternately, the Low-Income Housing Tax Credit has been slowly but surely gaining more provisions that establish preferences for proposals with certain characteristics, including geography. Why not a preference for tax credit projects in smart growth developments, where low-income

residents can share in the beautiful and unique communities being created?[42]

In addition, in order to convince investors that the proposed project is viable, developers should provide detailed documentation referring to mixed-use developments and walkable urban projects that have been completed and are considered successful. Market and consumer research studies should be used as well, to demonstrate that there is public demand for the new kind of built environment the new urbanists are proposing. With the purpose of making "walkable urbanism" legal, predictable permitting processes and fast-tracking permitting should be implemented as an incentive for mixed-use developments. Finally, coalition building with government, neighborhood groups, and environmental organizations should be established to help implement the solutions identified.[43]

Notes

1. See R. Steuteville, New Urbanism rocks, despite sluggish national economy. *New Urban News*, 2002, p.1, quoted in S. Deitrick& C. Ellis, New Urbanism in the Inner City, *Journal of American Planning Association*, 70(4): 426-442, 2004.

2. D. Brain, From Good Neighborhoods to Sustainable Cities: Social Science and the Social Agenda of New Urbanism, International Regional Science Review 28(2): 217-238, 2005, p. 218.

3. C. Ellis, The New Urbanism: Critiques and Rebuttals, *Urban Design*, 7(3): 261-291, 2002.

4. A. Njoh, New Urbanism, an Alternative to Traditional Urban Design: The Case of Celebration, Florida, USA (Case study prepared for *Revisiting Urban Planning: Global Report on Human Settlements* 2009), http://www.unhabitat.org/grhs/2009.

5. Njoh, *op. cit.*

6. Ellis, *op. cit.*

7. J. I. Gilderbloom, *Invisible City: Poverty, Housing, and New Urbanism* (Austin Texas: University Press of Texas, 2008).

8. See Louisville Development Bancorp Inc., Annual Mission Report, 2005.

9. http://www.trulia.com/KY/Louisville,3356,Park_Duvalle.

10. Ellis, *op. cit.*

11. D. Brain, *op. cit.*

12. Njoh, *op. cit.*

13. Gilderbloom, *op. cit.*

14. Njoh, *op. cit.*, p. 11.

15. See B. Hillier, Cities as Movement Economies, *Urban Design International*, 1(1): 41-60, 1996.

16. See The American Institute of Architects, The Village of Park DuValle: Project Details, http://www.aia.org/akr/Resources/Projects/AIAB081250.

17 . S.S. Fainstein, New Directions in Planning theory, *Urban Affairs Review*, 35(4): 451-478, 2000.

18. Fainstein, *op. cit.*, p. 464.

19. See Ellis, *op. cit.*

20. L. S. Sobel, W. Anderson and J. Shipman, *Market Acceptance of Smart Growth* (Washington, D. C.: US Environmental Protection Agency, 2011); http://bettercities.net/sites/default/files/market_acceptance_0.pdf.

21. C. Leinberger, The Death of the Fringe Suburb, *The New York Times*, No. 14, November 25, 2011.

22. Leinberger, *op.cit.*

23. See Ellis, *op. cit.*

24.C. Kennedy, The City of 2050 — An Age-Friendly, Vibrant Intergenerational Community, *Generations* 34(4): 70-75.

25. Leinberger, *op.cit.*

26. C. B. Leinberger and M. Alfonzo, Walk this Way: The Economic Promise of Walkable Places in Metropolitan Washington, D.C. (Washington, D.C. : The Brookings Institution) http://www.brookings.edu/~/media/research/files/papers/2012/5/25%20walkable%20places%20leinberger/25%20walkable%20places%20leinberger.pdf.

27. Gilderbloom, *op. cit.* p. 10-11. The author describes the application of the new urbanism paradigm to a poor, black neighborhood in west Louisville, KY. Through a partnership with the University of Louisville, developers were able to create affordable housing for more than one hundred homeowners and provided other residents with 550 housing rental units, without displacing any person. Through this revitalization project new businesses started to operate in the area, job opportunities were created, and the crime level decreased.

28. S. Khimm, Americans hate regulations in the abstract, but love them in particular, *The Washington Post*, 3/13/2012.

29. In Fainstein, *op. cit.,* p. 463.

30. Ellis, *op.cit.*, p 264.

31. See K. B. Silbaugh, Women's Place: Urban Planning, Housing Design, and Work-Family Balance, *Fordham Law Review,* 76, Boston University, School of Law Working Paper No. 07-12, 2008.

32. R.E. Lang, J. LeFurgy, and S. Homburg, *From Wall Street to Your Street: New Solutions for Smart Growth Finance* (Coral Gables, FL: Funders' Network for Smart Growth and Livable Communities, 2005), p. 20.

33. J. Jacobs, *The Death and Life of Great American Cities* (New York: Vintage Books, 1961).

34. Lang et al.,*op. cit.*

35. C. B. Leinberger & S. Kavage, Barriers to Developing Walkable Urbanism and Possible Solutions (Washington, DC: The Brookings Institution, 2007), http://chrisleinberger.com/docs/By_CL/Brookings_Barriers_05302007.pdf.

36. C. B. Leinberger, *Financing Progressive Developments* (Washington, DC: The Brookings Institution, 2001) http://www.brookings.edu/~/media/research/files/articles/2001/5/metropolitanpolicy%20leinberger/leinberger.

37. Lang et al.,*op. cit.*

38.Leinberger& Alfonzo, *op. cit.* p.2.

39. See Leinberger, 2001, p. 8 for a description of the 19 standardized real estate products.

40. Leinberger & Alfonzo, *op. cit.* p.2.

41. C. B. Leinberger, *The Option of Urbanism: Investing in a New American Dream* (Washington, D.C.: Island Press, 2009).

42. Lang et al.,*op. cit.,*p.22.

43. See Leinberger & Kavage, *op. cit.* for a more detailed presentation of potential solutions to different barriers encountered by new urbanism developers.

Selected Bibliography

Audirac, Ivonne. "Stated Preference for Pedestrian Proximity: An Assessment of New Urbanist Sense of Community." *Journal of Planning Education and Research* 19, no. 1 (1999): 53-66.

Audretsch, D. (1992). Reviews.*Kyklos*, *45*(2), 294. Retrieved from Academic Search Premier database.

Bates, Tim. "Michael Porter's Conservative Urban Agenda Will Not Revitalize "America's Inner Cities: What Will?." *Economic Development Quarterly*, Vol. 11 (1997). 39-54. Retrieved from Academic Search Premier database.

Bianco, M.J. "Robert Moses and Lewis Mumford: Competing Paradigms of Growth in Portland, Oregon." *Planning Perspectives*, 2001, 16: 95–114.

Bischoff, Dan. "Behind the Preservation Front," *Louisville Magazine*, January 1976, p.51

Blakely, E. and Snyder, M.G. *Fortress America: Gated Communities in the United States,* (Washington D.C: Brookings Institute Press, 1997).

Bookchin, M. *The Limits of the City.* Second Edition. Montreal: Black Rose Books, 1991.

Brain, D. "From Good Neighborhoods to Sustainable Cities: Social Science and the Social Agenda of New Urbanism." *International Regional Science Review* 28(2): 217-238, 2005, p. 218.

Brown, Barbara B. and Cropper, Vivian R. "New Urban and Standard Suburban Subdivisions: Evaluating Psychological and Social Goals." *Journal of the American Planning Association* 67, no. 4 (2001): 402-420.

Brüderl, J., Preisendörfer, P. and Ziegler, R. "Survival Chances of Newly Founded Business Organizations," *American Sociological Review*, Vol. 57, No 2, (1992) 227-242. Retrieved from Academic Search Premier database.

Bureau of the Census. *2011 Census Report-Summary Census Demographic Information.* Available at http://census/report.aspx.

Caro, Robert A. *The Power Broker: Robert Moses and the Fall of New York.* New York: Alfred A. Knopf, 1974.

Calthorpe, P. *The Next American Metropolis: Ecology, Community, and the American Dream* . NJ: Princeton Architectural Press, 1994.

Choldin, H.M. "Retrospective Review Essay: Neighborhood Life and Urban Environment." *American Journal of Sociology* 84(2), 1978, 457-463.

Former Secretaries, U.S. Department of Housing and Urban Development (HUD) Henry Cisneros and Shawn Donovan, *From Despair to Hope: Two HUD Secretaries on Urban Revitalization and Opportunity.* The Brookings Institution. Conference Presentation on July 14th, 2009, Washington D.C.

Cox, M.G. (1974). Economic, political and social developments since World War II. In J. B. Opdyke (Ed.), *Alachua County: A Sesquicentennial Tribute.* Gainesville, FL: The Alachua County Historical Commission, pp. 47.

Crowe, David. "The Information Source for the Home Building Industry. "Shifting Down: Are Smaller Homes a Permanent Trend?," (Cited October 16th, 2009). Available at http://www.builderonline.com/housing-trends/shifting-down. aspx.

Deere, as quoted in Harris, M. (2007, August 9). Haile Village Center brings residents and businesses together with New Urbanism concept. *The Gainesville Sun.* Retrieved from http://www.gainesville.com/article/20070809/NEWS/708090305? Title=Haile-Village-Center-brings-residents-and-businesses-together-with-New-Urbanism-concept.

Demerath, Loren, and Levinger, David. "The Social Qualities of Being on Foot: A Theoretical Analysis of Pedestrian Activity, Community, and Culture." *City & Community* 2, no. 3 (2003): 217-237.

Dickens, Charles. *A Tale of Two Cities*, (London: Oxford University Press).

Dorman, R.J. *Revolt of the Provinces: The Regionalist Movement in America 1920-1945* (University of North Carolina Press, 1993, p. 227).

Dreier, P. "Jane Jacobs' Radical Legacy." *Shelterforce Online*, Issue 146, Summer 2006. Available at: http://www.nhi.org/online/issues/146/janejacobslegacy.html.

Drylie, S. (1974). Alachua County, 1880-1900. In J. B. Opdyke (Ed.), *Alachua County: A Sesquicentennial Tribute*. Gainesville, FL: The Alachua County Historical Commission.

Duany, Andres, Plater-Zyberk, Elizabeth, and Speck, John. *Suburban Nation: The Rise of Sprawl and the Decline of the American Dream*, New York: North Point Press, 2000.

Fainstein, Susan. "New Directions in Planning Theory." *Urban Affairs Review*, 2000, 35(4): 451-478.

Federal Financial Institutions Examination Council, *2010 Census Reports-Summary Census Demographic Information*. Available at http://www.ffiec.gov/Geocode/CensusDemo.aspx.

Fjortoft, I. and Sageie, J. "The natural environment as a playground for children: Landscape description and analyses of a natural playscape." *Landscape and Urban Planning* 48: 83-97, 2000.

Florida, Richard. *The Rise of the Creative Class*, (New York: Basic Books, 2002).

Freeman, Lance. "The Effects of Sprawl on Neighborhood Social Ties." *Journal of the American Planning Association* 67, no. 1 (2001): 69-77.

Garde, Ajay. "Designing and Developing New Urbanist Projects in the United States: Insights and Implications." *Journal of Urban Design* Vol. 11, No. 1, (2006): 33-54.

Geoghegan, John. "The Value of Open Spaces in Residential Land Use." *Land Use Policy* 19, no. 1: 91-98, 2002.

Gilderbloom, John I. *Invisible City: Poverty, Housing, and New Urbanism* Austin Texas: University Press of Texas, 2008.

Hillier, B. "Cities as Movement Economies." *Urban Design International*, 1(1): 41-60, 1996.

———. E. House, and M. Hanka, "Historic Preservation in Kentucky." Preservation Kentucky, Inc. (2007).

Glaab, C. N. and Brown, A. T. *A History of Urban America*, Third Edition. New York: Macmillan & Co., 1983.

———. Uncommon Sense: Remembering Jane Jacobs, who Wrote the 20th Century Most Influential Book about Cities. The American Scholar, Autumn 2006. Avaialble at http://theamericanscholar.org/uncomon-sense/

Goldschmidt quoted in *A Tribute to Lewis Mumford* (Cambridge, MA: Lincoln Institute of Land Policy, 1982), pp. 16, 21: interview with Perry Norton, 1988.

Grant, John. *Planning the Good Community: New Urbanism in Theory and Practice*. London: Routledge, 2006.

Hart, S. and Spivak, A. *The Elephant in the Bedroom: Automobile Dependence and Denial; Impacts on the Economy and Environment*, Pasadena, CA: New Paradigm Books, 1993.

Harvey, David. "The New Urbanism and the Communitarian Trap," *Harvard Design Magazine*, Winter/Spring 1997: 1-3.

Jacobs, Jane. *The Death and Life of Great American Cities,* (New York: Vintage Books, 1961.

Katz, P. *The New Urbanism: Toward an Architecture of Community* New York: McGraw-Hill, 1994.

Kennedy, C. "The City of 2050 — An Age-Friendly, Vibrant Intergenerational Community." *Generations* 34(4): 70-75.

Kim, Joongsub and Kaplan, Rachel. "Physical and Psychological Factors in Sense of Community: New Urbanist Kentlands and Nearby Orchard Village." *Environment and Behavior* 36, no. 3 (2004): 313-340.

Kirchoff, B.A. *Entrepreneurship and Dynamic Capitalism.* Westport, CT: Praeger, 1994.

Klemek, C. "Dead or Alive at Fifty?" Reading Jane Jacobs on her Golden Anniversary, *Dissent,* 58(2), 2011, 75-79.

———. op. cit.; M. Lind, Urban Philosopher: A Walking Tour of Lewis Mumford, December 30, 1999, *New America Foundation,* http://newamerica.net/node/5660.

Kramer, R. *Breaking the Habit of Suburbia.* Atlanda, Georgia. February 11, 2001. Presentation. Retrieved from http://www.webenet.com/newurbanism.htm

Kunstler, J.H. *Home from Nowhere: Remaking Our Everyday World for the Twenty-first Century,* New York: Simon and Schuster, 1996.

Kuo, Frances E., Sullivan, Coley, William C., Rebekah, L., and Brunson, Liesette. "Fertile Ground for Community: Inner-City Neighborhood Common Spaces." *American Journal of Community Psychology,* 26, no. 6, (1998): 823-851.

LaCoe, N. (1974). The Alachua frontier. In J. B. Opdyke (Ed.), *Alachua County: A Sesquicentennial Tribute.* Gainesville, FL: The Alachua County Historical Commission.

Lang, Robert E., LeFurgy, J., and Homburg, S. *From Wall Street to Your Street: New Solutions for Smart Growth Finance.* Coral Gables, FL: Funders' Network for Smart Growth and Livable Communities, 2005.

Lawrence, P.L. The Unknown Jane Jacobs: Geographer, Propagandist, City Planning Idealist (pp. 15-36). In Page, M. & Mennel, T. (eds.) Reconsidering Jane Jacobs, (Washington, D. C.: APA Planners Press, 2011).

Leinberger, C.B. *Financing Progressive Developments* (Washington, DC: The Brookings Institution,   2001)   http://www.brookings.edu/~/media/research/files/articles/2001/5/metropolitanpolicy%20leinberger/leinberger

———. *The Next Slum?* (The Atlantic Online, March, 2008.

———. *The Option of Urbanism: Investing in a New American Dream* (Washington, D.C.: Island Press, 2009).

———. and Alfonzo, M. Walk this Way: The Economic Promise of Walkable Places in Metropolitan Washington, D.C. (Washington, D.C. : The Brookings Institution) http://www.brookings.edu/~/media/research/files/papers/2012/5/25%20walkable%20places%20leinberger/25%20walkable%20places%20leinberger.pdf.

———. and S. Kavage, Barriers to Developing Walkable Urbanism and Possible Solutions (Washington, DC: The Brookings Institution, 2007), http://chrisleinberger.com/docs/By_CL/Brookings_Barriers_05302007.pdf.

Levine, M., Perkins, D.D. and Perkins, D. *Principles of Community Psychology: Perspectives and Applications, 3rd ed.* New York: Oxford University Press, 2005.

Levy, John. *Contemporary Urban Planning 8th ed.* New Jersey: Pearson Prentice-Hall, 2009.

Lind, M. Urban Philosopher: A Walking Tour of Lewis Mumford, December 30, 1999, New America Foundation, http://newamerica.net/node/5660.

Liu, Ben-Chien *Quality of Life Indicators in U.S. Metropolitan Areas: A Statistical Analysis* New York: Praeger, 1976.
Louisville Development Bancorp Inc., Annual Mission Report, 2005. http://www.trulia.com/KY/Louisville,3356,Park_Duvalle.
Luccarelli, M. *Lewis Mumford and the Ecological Region: The Politics of Planning* New York, NY: The Guilford Press, 1995.
Lund, Hollie. "Pedestrian Environments and Sense of Community." *Journal of Planning Education and Research* 21, no. 3 (2002): 301-312.
Market Segments: Potential Demand and Product Opportunities. Report Prepared for the City of Carmel by Jackson Research and Consulting, June, 2009.
Miller, D. L. *Lewis Mumford: A Life.* New York: Weidenfeld and Nicolson, 1989.
Miller, Z.A. and Melvin, P.A. *The Urbanization of Modern America. A Brief History.* Second Edition. New York: Harcourt Brace Jovanovich, Publishers, 1987.
Mumford, Lewis. *The City in History.* New York: Harvest Books, 1961.
———. *The Culture of Cities* (New York: Harcourt, Brace and Company, 1938).
———. Home Remedies for Urban Cancer, in L. K. Loewenstein (ed.) *Urban Studies. An Introductory Reader.* (New York: The Free Press, 1971, 385-404).
Naisbitt, John. *High Tech, High Touch.* New York: Broadway Books, 1999.
Nasar, Jack and Julian, David A. "The Psychological Sense of Community in the Neighborhood." *Journal of the American Planning Association* 61, no. 2 (1995): 178-184.
New Urbanism News (n.d.) Accessed December 15th, 2004. http://www.newurbanismnews.com/,
Newman, Oscar. *Defensible Space: Crime Prevention Through Urban Design.* New York: Collier Books, 1969.
Njoh, A. New Urbanism, an Alternative to Traditional Urban Design: The Case of Celebration, Florida, USA (Case study prepared for *Revisiting Urban Planning: Global Report on Human Settlements* 2009), http://www.unhabitat.org/grhs/2009.
Osborne, David and Gaebler, Ted. *Reinventing Government: How the Entrepreneurial Spirit is Transforming the Public Sector.* New York: Penguin Books, 1992.
Palen, J.J. *The Urban World, Third Edition.* New York: McGrow - Hill Book Company, 1987.
Parsons, K.C. Collaborative Genius: The Regional Planning Association of America, *Journal of the American Planning Association,* 1994, 60(4): 462-482.
Parsons, K. C and Schuyler, D. eds., *From Garden City to Green City: The Legacy of Ebenezer Howard.* Baltimore: The Johns Hopkins University Press, 2002.
Perry, D. and Wiewel, W. *The University as Urban Developer: Case Studies and Analysis,* Armonk, NY: M.E.Sharpe, 2005.
Phillips, B.D. and Kirchoff, B.A. "Formation, Growth, and Survival: Small Firm Dynamics in the U.S. Economy." *Small Business Economics,* Vol. 1, (1989) 65–74.
Picard, John B. *Florida's Eden — An Illustrated History of Alachua County,* (Gainesville, FL: Maupin House, 1994); Ellerbe, H.C. (1974). Statehood, Secession and Reconstruction. In J. B. Opdyke (Ed.), *Alachua County: A Sesquicentennial Tribute.* Gainesville, FL: The Alachua County Historical Commission.
Plas, Jeanne M and Lewis, Susan E. "Environmental Factors and Sense of Community in a Planned Town," *American Journal of Community Psychology* 24, no. 1 (1996): 109-143.
Porter, Michael E. "The Competitive Advantage of the Inner City." *Harvard Business Review,* May-June, (1995). 55-71. Retrieved from Academic Search Premier database.

Price, Michael (2006). *Old Louisville by the Numbers: A Statistical Profile.* Available at http://srvr18.ud.net/downloads/olcc/Old_Louisville_May_06.ppt.

Rowe, Robert (2010, November 21). [Letter to Wes White]. Retrieved from http://www.hailewest.org.

Rubin, T.S. "Countering the Rhetoric of Emerging Domestic Markets: Why More Information Alone Will Not Address the Capital Needs of Underserved Areas." *Economic Development Quarterly,* Vol. 25, No. 2, (2012) 182-192. Retrieved from Academic Search Premier database.

Rypkema. D. "Preservation and Property Values in Indiana." Historic Landmarks Foundation of Indiana. (1997).

———. "Smart Growth, Sustainable Development and Historic Preservation." Presentation at the Bridging Boundaries-Building Great Communities Regional Smart Growth Conference, Louisville, KY, September 19th, 2006; and R. Florida, *The Rise of the Creative Class.* New York: Basic Books, 2002.

Silbaugh, K.B. "Women's Place: Urban Planning, Housing Design, and Work-Family Balance." *Fordham Law Review,* 76, Boston University, School of Law Working Paper No. 07-12, 2008.

Skjaeveland, Oddvar. "Effects of Street Parks on Social Interactions Among Neighbors: A Place Perspective," *Journal of Architectural and Planning Research* 18, no. 2 (2001): 131-147.

Shands HealthCare (2010). *Shands HealthCare and the University of Florida health Science Center 2010 Community Benefit Report.* Retrieved from http://www.shands.org/about/community benefit/2010/default.asp.

Spencer, A.P. (1974). The World Wars. In J. B. Opdyke (Ed.), *Alachua County: A Sesquicentennial Tribute.*Gainesville, FL: The Alachua County Historical Commission.

Sperling, B. and Sander, P. *Cities Ranked & Rated Second Edition.* (Hoboken, NJ: Wiley Publishing, Inc., 2007.

Steuteville, R. New Urbanism rocks, despite sluggish national economy. *New Urban News,* 2002, p.1, quoted in S. Deitrick & C. Ellis, New Urbanism in the Inner City, *Journal of American Planning Association,* 70(4): 426-442, 2004.

K.R. Stunkel, *Understanding Lewis Mumford: A Guide for the Perplexed.* Lewiston, N.Y.: The Edwin Mellon Press, 2004.

Sullivan, Jenny. "Custom Home Magazine. "Home Prices Continue to Shrink." (Cited January 22nd, 2010).Accessed July 5th http://www.customhome online.com/industry-news.

Sunnyside Gardens Historic District Designation Report (New York City Landmarks Preservation Commission, June 26, 2007; http://www.landmarkwatch.org/PDF/2SunnysideGardens.pdf).

Tae-Kyung, K. Horner, M. W. and. Marans, R. W. "Life cycle and environmental factors in selecting residential and job locations." *Housing Studies* 20, no. 3: 457-73, 2005.

Talen, E. "Measuring the Public Realm: A Preliminary Assessment of the Link Between Public Space and Sense of Community," *Journal of Architectural and Planning Research* 17, no. 4 (2000): 344-360.

———. Beyond the Front Porch: Regionalist Ideals in the New Urbanist Movement, *Journal of Planning History,* 2008 vol. 7(1), pp. 20-47, p. 20.

———. *New Urbanism and American Planning: The Conflict of Cultures,* (New York: Routledge, 2005).

The American Institute of Architects, The Village of Park DuValle: Project Details, http://www.aia.org/akr/Resources/Projects/AIAB081250.

Thomas, S.W. *Cherokee Triangle: A History of the Heart of the Highlands,* (Louisville, KY: Butler Book Publishing, 2003).

Wendt, M. "The Importance of Death and Life of the American Great Cities (1961) by Jane Jacobs to the Profession of Urban Planning." *New Visions for Public Affairs,* Vol. 1, Spring 2009, pp. 1-24.

White, S. and Ellis, C. "Sustainability, the Environment, and New Urbanism: An Assessment and Agenda for Research," *Journal of Architectural and Planning Research,* Vol. 24, No. 2 (2007): 125-142.

Wiewel, W. and Knaap, G. *Partnership for Smart Growth: University-Community Collaboration for Better Public Places.* Armonk, NY: M.E. Sharpe, 2005.

Wojtowicz, R. "City As Community: The Life And Vision of Lewis Mumford." *Quest,* January 2001, 4 (1), 1-4.

———. Review of Mumford, Lewis, *The Culture of Cities.* H-Urban, H-Net Reviews. January, 1999. http://www.h-net.org/reviews/showrev.php?id=266.